RELIGION AND ECONOMIC ACTION

A Critique of Max Weber

hArpER ☘ ᴛorchbooks

EDITORS' NOTE: *A check-list of Harper Torchbooks, classified by subjects, is printed at the end of this volume.*

RESEARCHES IN THE SOCIAL, CULTURAL AND BEHAVIORAL SCIENCES

edited by Benjamin Nelson

RELIGION AND
ECONOMIC ACTION

A Critique of Max Weber

KURT SAMUELSSON

TRANSLATED FROM THE SWEDISH
BY
E. GEOFFREY FRENCH

EDITED AND WITH AN INTRODUCTION BY
D. C. COLEMAN

HARPER TORCHBOOKS ❦ The Academy Library
Harper & Row, Publishers
New York and Evanston

Every rich man regards wealth as a personal
attribute. And so does every poor man. Everyone is tacitly convinced of it. Only logic makes
some difficulties by asserting that the possession of money may perhaps confer certain
qualities, but can never itself be a human
quality. Closer inspection gives this the lie . .
. . . . . . Destroy bank account and credit, and
not only has the rich man no money left, but
on the day when he realises this he is a with-
ered flower.

ROBERT MUSIL, *The Man Without Qualities*

2677

RELIGION AND ECONOMIC ACTION

© 1957 Kurt Samuelsson
English translation © 1961 E. Geoffrey French

Printed in the United States of America.

This book was originally published in Sweden in 1957 under the title *Ekonomi och religion*. The English translation was published in the United States by Basic Books in 1961, and is here reprinted by arrangement.

First HARPER TORCHBOOK edition published 1964 by
Harper & Row, Publishers, Incorporated
49 East 33rd Street
New York 16, N.Y.

Introduction

Historical controversy is the life-blood of historical writing. Without it, history becomes dogma. To the layman the process of controversy may sometimes appear as a peevish squabble of pedants, and to the professionals variously as a disturbing revelation of X's carelessness, Y's bad temper or Z's tendency to make his generalisations too bold to be good. But if history is to remain alive it must secure at least periodic freedom from the lethal benedictions of accepted authority. And whatever may have happened to Max Weber's theories about the influence upon economic life of Protestantism in general and Puritanism in particular, nobody could say they were dead or claim that they had passed unchallenged or unsupported. It is a tribute to the continuing fascination of the subject that in half a century it should have attracted contributions from many countries: Sombart and Brentano in Germany, Robertson and Tawney in England, Fanfani in Italy, Talcott Parsons in America—to mention only a few of the better-known names.

The very fact of the continuing influence of Weber's hypotheses is in itself a tribute, be it to their truth or to some deep-seated appeal which they possess. For in spite of much damaging criticism, of refutations and counter-refutations, the belief in some sort of influence wielded by Puritanism on capitalism is still strong and pervasive. At the present time it is probably more in favour in the United States than in Britain, and perhaps more amongst historically-minded sociologists than amongst historians. But this is partly a matter of degree and of timing. For there can be little doubt that much of this continuing influence emanates from that generalized and modified version

v

of Weber's original thesis which is so brilliantly expounded in the outstanding English contribution to the debate: R. H. Tawney's *Religion and the Rise of Capitalism*. Of all the contributions it is almost certainly the best-known and undoubtedly the most strikingly written; more than any other work it has carried the generalized idea of a positive relation between Puritanism and capitalism out of the private world of specialists into the public world of the general reader.

Dr Samuelsson's book is the first major discussion of the subject to come from Sweden and the latest entrant to the lists. The author is an economic historian whose publications include a study of the Stockholm merchant houses in the 18th century and a history of the big Stockholm department store, N.K. (Nordiska Kompaniet), as well as various articles, some of which have appeared in English;[1] he is also known to a wider public in Sweden as an active journalist, and for his commentaries on current affairs on radio and television. The present work was published in Swedish in 1957 under the title *Ekonomi och Religion*. It will have none of Weber and little of Tawney. A bold and hard-hitting essay in interpretation rather than a detailed monograph, it asks the central question: was there any connection between Protestantism and economic progess? 'Did such a clear correlation,' he asks, 'exist between Protestantism and economic progress that there is any reason to enquire into cause and effect at all?'

Not everyone will concur with what Dr Samuelsson has to say nor, I am sure, would he wish them to. But the cold water which he showers with refreshing gusto on the notion of a functional relationship between capitalism and religious faith as such should disturb, with admirable discomfort, the too ready

---

[1] *De Stora Köpmanshusen i Stockholm, 1730—1815* and *Nordiska Kompaniet, historien om ett varuhus* appeared in 1951 and 1952 respectively. Articles in English include 'International Payments and Credit Movements by the Swedish Merchant Houses, 1730—1815' and 'The Banks and the Financing of Industry in Sweden, c. 1900—1927' in the *Scandinavian Economic History Review*, Vol. III, No. 2, 1955 and Vol. VI, No. 2, 1958 respectively.

slumbers of accepted abstractions. Puritan thrift and economic success, Protestantism and Capitalism, Catholicism and—what shall it be?—absence of the 'capitalistic spirit': anyone disposed to the making of such marriages should, after reading Dr Samuelsson's book, be better equipped to ponder the significance of the following observations. The first was made by a Catholic Frenchman, with positivistic and utilitarian leanings and a sympathy for Anglicanism, whilst visiting England in the heyday of its economic success:

'To earn a lot consume a lot—such is the rule. The Englishman does not save money, does not think of the future; at most he will insure his life. He is the reverse of the Frenchman, who is frugal and "abstemious".'[2]

The second surely breathes the very air of 'Puritan' devotion to thrift, diligence, capitalism and the business life:

'When a man has capital, small though it may be, he must allow himself no relaxation in his attention to household problems or the running of his business, and must continue to make the earning of a living his principal concern. This is his lifelong duty. If, when one has capital, one begins to relax, to buy things one longs for, to behave in a wilful manner, to live in style, and to do all the things which one wishes to do, the money is soon spent.... One must set to work from the moment one has capital.'

These admonitions to hard work do, it is true, date from the early 17th century, 1610 to be precise. But they come from Japan, and it seems unlikely that their author was moved by Calvinistic zeal. He was, indeed, at pains to emphasise that the last thing for economic success is religion:

[2] Hippolyte Taine in 1862. See *Taine's Notes on England* (translated by Edward Hyams, London, 1957, p. 26).

'It is forbidden to worry about the after-life until you have reached the age of fifty. Such thoughts are for old men only, or for members of the Jōdo or Zen sects. For anyone else they are a waste of time. Above all, conversion to Christianity is forbidden . . . . Christianity is the greatest of afflictions for a man whose concern is the management of a household.' [3]

Perhaps the relations between Christianity and capitalism need to be looked at from viewpoints rather different from those customarily adopted in the past. By its vigorous scepticism Dr Samuelsson's book will help us to find them.

*

A brief word should perhaps be said about the relation of this English edition to the original Swedish text. After Mr French had translated the latter I made a number of amendments to that translation. These consisted mainly of changes of sequence, emphasis or reference, designed to make the final version appropriate to English or English-speaking readers. I have also added a number of explanatory points to the footnotes. Mr. French and I have jointly tried to retain wherever possible something of the pungent flavour of the style in which the original was written. With what success readers must judge.

Finally, both Mr French and Dr Samuelsson join me in gratefully acknowledging a debt of thanks to Professor E. F. Söderlund of Stockholm for his help in bringing about this English edition and his assistance on various points of detail.

London, 1959   D. C. COLEMAN

[3] 'Shimai Sōshitsu no Yuikun Jūshichi-ka-jō' (The Seventeen Injunctions of Shimai Sōshitsu), in *The Japanese Family Storehouse or the Millionaires' Gospel Modernised* (translated by G. W. Sargent, Cambridge, 1959, Appendix 3, pp. 245 and 249). I am indebted to my colleague Professor Henry Phelps Brown for drawing my attention to this fascinating work.

Contents

Author's Foreword

The suggestion for the topic of this book is my own—but not the suggestion that I should write a book on the topic. In the spring of 1955 I mentioned to Professor Herbert Tingsten that I was engaged in writing a short essay on Max Weber and his ideas on Protestantism and capitalism. It was intended to be included in a symposium of essays on economic history that was then being planned. He urged me to write a separate book on the topic instead.

Here it is. While writing it I have many times discussed with Herbert Tingsten the problems it posed and the 'discoveries' I thought I had made. I need not elaborate on the value these discussions have had for my work. I have real cause to be grateful to him.

The critical appraisal of Dr Olof Lagercrantz and Dr Karl-Erik Lundevall afforded me much help; I would add that without the encouragement of Olof Lagercrantz, the burden of completing the task would have weighed much more heavily.

During a stay in England in the autumn of 1955 I had the opportunity of discussing various problems touched upon in the book with, among others, Professors R. H. Tawney and T. S. Ashton, both of whom are frequently mentioned in the course of my exposition. I did not, of course, conceal that I found myself in disagreement with both these English scholars on fundamental aspects of this topic and that I intended to criticise their results. This did not prevent either of them from displaying a most generous readiness to lend me their aid.

Nacka, May 1957   KURT SAMUELSSON

CHAPTER I

The Problem and the Controversy

1. WEBER'S HYPOTHESES

Max Weber published his study of Protestantism and Capitalism in 1905.[1] Ever since there has been controversy about the impact of religious belief on the economic actions of mankind. Was it religion, the doctrines of Protestantism, that impelled men to economic achievement? Were the Protestant states more successful economically than the Catholic and, if so, does religion provide the explanation and cause of this difference? Would 'capitalism', that powerful economic advance which surged across northern and western Europe and later America,

---

[1] *Die Protestantische Ethik und der Geist des Kapitalismus* was first published in the *Archiv für Sozialwissenschaft und Sozialpolitik*, Vols. XX and XXI, 1904—5. Reprinted in 1920 in the *Gesammelte Aufsätze zur Religionssoziologie*, with certain revisions, and in particular an appropriate body of footnotes, it was first published in Great Britain in 1930 as *The Protestant Ethic and the Spirit of Capitalism*, in a translation by Talcott Parsons and with a Foreword by R. H. Tawney. Included in these *Gesammelte Aufsätze* is also an additional study entitled *Die Protestantische Sekten und der Geist des Kapitalismus* which surprisingly was not incorporated in the English edition. All specific references given here to the *Protestant Ethic* (cited hereafter as such) are to the English edition, though Dr. Samuelsson's references to the *Gesammelte Aufsätze zur Religionssoziologie* (referred to hereafter as *Gesammelte Aufsätze*) have also been retained. Cf. E. Fischoff, 'The Protestant Ethic and the Spirit of Capitalism', *Social Research*, No. 11 (1944), pp. 53—77. See also M. Weber's *Gesammelte Aufsätze zur Wirtschaftslehre* (1922) and *Wirtschaft und Gesellschaft* (Part. I: 3 in *Grundriss der Sozialökonomik*) (1925).

1

never have come into being had it not been for the doctrines of Protestantism?

Weber asserted strenuously that such causal links did indeed exist. Protestantism created the pre-conditions for a 'spirit of capitalism'. The dictum hardly applied to Lutheranism, which retained the traditional canonical attitude to trade. But it applied without reservation to Calvinism and the various Protestant sects. Weber contended, firstly, that a man's trade, or calling, constituted a religious mission in their eyes. The fulfilment of the daily task was a deed pleasing to God; success in one's trade was a mark of conduct deserving in His sight. These ideas promoted diligence. In Benjamin Franklin Weber finds the logical consequence of this outlook. Franklin, man of the Enlightenment, he sees as the foremost exponent of the 'spirit of capitalism'. Moral conceptions find in him an utilitarian anchorage; honesty is useful because it builds credit; therefore one ought to be honest. The second important characteristic of Calvinism and the Protestant sects Weber held to be the emphasis upon thrift. A notable thriftiness—pushed by the Puritans to sheer asceticism—combined with the concept of the fulfilment of earthly duty as the highest purpose in life, could not but bring about the formation of capital. Weber quotes the father of Methodism, John Wesley: 'Religion must necessarily produce both industry and frugality, and these cannot but produce riches'.[2]

Weber based his analysis upon conditions in certain German states which had mixed religious faiths. A study by Martin Offenbacher of the occupations of Catholics and Protestants in Baden, published in 1901,[3] served as his starting-point. Offenbacher believed he had succeeded in establishing that Protestants, more commonly than Catholics, sent their children to

[2] *Protestant Ethic*, p. 175.

[3] M. Offenbacher, *Konfession und soziale Schichtung. Eine Studie über die wirtschaftliche Lage der Katholiken und Protestanten in Baden* (1901), Vol. IV, part. V, of the *Volkswirtschaftliche Abhandlungen der badischen Hochschulen*.

'non-obligatory' high schools; and, moreover, that Protestant students, more commonly than Catholics, studied subjects especially suitable for future technicians and entrepreneurs. Weber declared, furthermore, that movement out of handicrafts and into skilled industrial trades was much more usual among Protestant than Catholic journeymen. The Catholics stayed in handicraft trades and became masters; the Protestants went into industry and became artisans. 'The explanation of these cases is undoubtedly that the mental and spiritual peculiarities (*die geistige Eigenart*) acquired from the environment, here the type of education favoured by the religious atmosphere of the home community and the parental home, have determined the choice of occupation, and through it the professional career'.[4]

The special competence in economic matters apparently displayed by particular groups has been attributed to the fact that these groups were politically and socially underprivileged: the Poles in Russia, Huguenots in the France of Louis XIV, Nonconformists and Quakers in England, and Jews virtually everywhere. They could not obtain state employment, they were oppressed and subordinated—and this might be thought to have compelled them to address themselves to business enterprise. But, says Weber, no such tendency is to be found amongst the Catholics in Germany; nor did the Catholics of England and the Netherlands reveal themselves, as subordinate groups, to be nurtured to habits of economic zeal. The hypothesis that the Protestants became economically skilful only when subordinated is quite mistaken. Both as minorities and as majorities, Protestant groups asserted themselves in economic affairs with conspicuous success. Weber sums up: 'Thus the principal explanation of this difference must be sought in the permanent intrinsic character of their religious beliefs, and not only in their temporary external historio-political situation.'[5] The problem to be studied, therefore, was to discover what elements in each faith worked, and to some extent still work, to these differing ends. And so he arrived at his thesis of Protestantism and the 'spirit

[4] *Protestant Ethic,* p. 39. [5] *Ibid.,* p. 40.

3

of capitalism' with its constituent elements—the 'calling', thrift, and 'rationalism'.

In his *Wirtschaftsgeschichte*,[6] Weber reiterated this thesis with even greater vigour. After various possibilities, including the theory of the role of the Jews launched by Sombart, have been firmly rejected, there at last remains only the Reformation. The foundation of the 'spirit of capitalism', unity and austerity in personal conduct, could not be laid by the Catholic church. That church had far too great an understanding of the essential dissonance of human nature, of the fact that people could be wicked and good at one and the same time. Through the confession and absolution of sins the light of its grace was permitted to shine over saint and sinner alike: 'The Reformation made a decisive break with this system.'[7] The sinner could no longer find forgiveness and atonement in renunciation and the monastic life. Only by fulfilling the daily call, by being indeed a monk in the everyday deeds of life, could salvation be won. 'Out of this system of thought,' Weber concludes, 'came our word "calling" (*Beruf*), which is known only to the languages influenced by the Protestant translations of the Bible.'[8]

2. THEIR CURRENT INFLUENCE

Weber's ideas came to exercise a great influence upon popular conceptions. They have been referred to as self-evident truths— more or less in passing and often without Weber himself being mentioned—in innumerable textbooks of history and sociology. People who have never heard of Weber, to whom his work is utterly unknown, have confidently asserted the importance of the impact of religion on economic life. It is a fine testimony to the truth of Lord Keynes' celebrated dictum: 'practical

[6] Put together from his lectures, 'Outlines of Universal Social and Economic History' given in Germany in 1919—20; translated into English by F. H. Knight and published as *General Economic History* in 1927. References here are to this English edition.

[7] *General Economic History*, p. 365. [8] *Ibid.*, p. 367.

4

men, who believe themselves to be quite exempt from any intellectual influences, are usually the slaves of some defunct economist.'[9]

But it has not been simply in these, so to speak, anonymous forms that Weber's theories have been propagated. Even in ambitious scholarly inquiries in the fields of sociology, ecclesiastical history, economic history and economic theory, they have insinuated themselves as coins of common currency, unreflectingly accepted as self-evident truths to be cited without being tested. Some examples from the last ten years may be mentioned.

No one has ever been able seriously to dispute Weber, writes H. E. Barnes in his *Historical Sociology*,[10] fifty years after the publication of *Die Protestantische Ethik*. Such criticisms as have been made have not upset his thesis in any essential respect. On the few points where at first sight criticism appears justified, says Barnes, it is in fact founded upon misunderstanding or exaggeration of what Weber said. Weber never said that Protestantism, particularly in its Calvinist form, was the only source of capitalism (implying, thereby, that someone *had* asserted that he had said this). Protestantism was in reality 'only' the decisive factor: 'Weber did not contend that Protestantism, especially Calvinism, was the sole cause of capitalism, which he regarded as having been produced by many factors, but he did hold that, without the Protestant Ethics, capitalism would not have made its apearance.'[11]

Talcott Parsons' contribution to the symposium, *An Introduction to the History of Sociology*,[12] exhibits exactly the same approach. Parsons is as ardent in defending Weber as he has been assiduous in translating him. In 1954 another American

[9] J. M. Keynes, *The General Theory of Employment, Interest and Money* (1936), p. 383.

[10] H. E. Barnes, *Historical Sociology: its Origins and Development* (1948), pp. 59—61. [11] *Ibid.*, p. 124.

[12] 'Max Weber's Sociological Analysis of Capitalism and Modern Institutions', in Barnes (Ed.) *An Introduction to the History of Sociology* (1948), pp. 287—308.

sociologist, Irwin G. Wyllie, attempted to apply Weber's thesis to American conditions.[13] Wyllie finds that Weber was rather cautious. By so strongly emphasising the importance of the secular component in Benjamin Franklin's attitude, Weber, it seems, retreated much too far from the basic concept of the importance of religious belief.

The position taken up on Weber by Eli F. Heckscher, with his great scholarly authority in economic history, both in Sweden and internationally, is of considerable interest. Heckscher ranked Weber very high. Weber, he wrote, was 'together with Marx, the only great talent produced by Germany in the field of true sociological scholarship.' He specially praised Weber for taking note, like Sombart, of the causes of change in the human mentality: 'It is in this field that some of the greatest achievements of Max Weber and Sombart lie.' It is true that at one point of the discussion whether it was Protestantism that modified economic thought or economic changes that influenced both economic and religious thought, Heckscher seems almost to demur from the Weber thesis. Presumably, he declares, the Enlightenment furnished a common denominator. And admittedly diligence was more vigorously encouraged in Catholic France than in Protestant England. But, he stresses in another context, by so zealously calling attention to the Puritans' and particularly the Quakers', ideal of thrift, Weber makes a massive contribution to the elucidation of the history of capital and capitalism. Allowance must be made, as a matter of principle, for the impact on economies of non-economic forces. 'And this is what has been done, for example, in the most celebrated and stimulating contributions to the study of what is called the rise of modern capitalism (viz., Weber's and Sombart's).' Heckscher particularly singles out Weber in this connection: 'Here it was the stamp that Protestantism received through—at least in part—ethical, religious, non-economic causes that transformed the economy itself and thereby contributed to laying the foundations

[13] I. G. Wyllie, *The Self-Made Man in America: the Myth of Rags to Riches* (1954).

6

of the 19th century economic system, unique in history.'[14]

In the course of his *Theory of Economic Growth* (1955) the distinguished economist, W. Arthur Lewis, considers, more than once, the problem of the influence of religion upon economic expansion. His views are summarised in a section entitled *Religion*. How compatible, he asks, is economic growth with various types of religious attitude? And secondly: do incompatible beliefs stifle growth, or is it merely that such beliefs flourish where the conditions for economic growth do not exist, and are rejected as soon as growth becomes possible? The first is easier to answer than the second, writes Lewis, after formulating these manifestly Weberesque questions.

What is Lewis' answer then? On the whole he considers religion, regardless of the form it takes, to be a hindrance. Most religions teach that it is better to devote oneself to spiritual contemplation rather than to an unrelenting striving after higher receipts and lower costs; practically all religions set their face against the appetite for material possessions. However, an exception should be made for the doctrines of Protestantism: 'Some religions do teach that salvation can be reached through the discipline of hard and conscientious work and do elevate the pursuit of efficiency into a moral virtue. Some forms of Christianity also lay emphasis upon the virtues of thrift, and of productive investment.' After some varied discussion, Lewis summarises his views thus: 'If a religion lays stress upon material values, upon work, upon thrift and productive investment, upon honesty in commercial relations, upon experimentation and risk-bearing, and upon equality of opportunity, it will be helpful to growth, whereas in so far as it is hostile to these things, it tends to inhibit growth.'[15]

[14] E. F. Heckscher, *Ekonomisk-historiska Studier* (1936), p. 13 ff.; *Historieuppfattning, materialistisk och annan* (1944), p. 20; *Industrialismen* (1948, 4th Ed.), pp. 10, 46; see also *Mercantilism* (2nd English Ed. 1955), Vol. II, pp. 154—5. All references to *Mercantilism* given here are to this English edition.

[15] W. A. Lewis, *The Theory of Economic Growth* (1955), pp. 101—7, esp. pp. 101, 105.

Gunnar Myrdal is of the same opinion. In his book, *An International Economy: Problems and Prospects,* he makes a passing reference to the significance of religion: 'The Protestant religion, in its Lutheran and still more in its Calvinist branches, retained comparatively little place for grace and indulgence and advanced a hard morality of efforts and deeds; it prompted a social spirit of individual responsibility and personal emulation, if not competition, and therefore gave a moral value to the individual's social and economic advance.'[16]

Even outside the domain of sociology and economics, we can find Weber quoted with acclamation and esteem. René Wellek and Austin Warren, the leaders of the new literary criticism in America, have an appreciative word in passing for Weber's philosophy of religion: 'Whatever their failure at isolating the religious factor, the studies of Max Weber in the sociology of religion are valuable for their attempt to describe the influence of ideological factors on economic behaviour and institutions, for earlier emphasis had been entirely upon the economic influence on ideology.'[17]

Half a century since his theories appeared in the *Archiv für Socialwissenschaft,* and Weber is still an author *à la mode.* Half a century of unparalleled economic progress, accompanied by universal secularisation, and yet there has been no thorough retesting of those theories. This is not because criticism has been lacking. On the contrary, his ideas have been vigorously discussed in a number of works, and some powerful objections have been raised.

3. THE CONTROVERSY

The first to bring Weber's theories into serious discussion was Felix Rachfahl. He launched his offensive in a series of articles, 'Kapitalismus und Kalvinismus,' in the *Internationale Wochen-*

[16] G. Myrdal, *International Economy: Problems and Prospects* (1956), p. 18.
[17] R. Wellek and A. Warren, *Theory of Literature* (1955), p. 104.

schrift für Wissenschaft, Kunst und Technik, four years after the publication of *Die Protestantische Ethik.* Rachfahl had what amounted to four main objections to Weber. All of them have, in one form or another, since reappeared in the writings of other authors.

Firstly: the very idea of an ethical-religious motivation, as something specially important in economic activity, is dubious. The driving forces that operate may derive from entirely different motives, 'such as the desire to enjoy life, solicitude for the family, the urge to work for one's fellow-man, for the common good, for the nation and its welfare. They may also be associated with a special ethical doctrine of a «calling," but they may equally stand in direct opposition to the generally accepted tenets of the period and people.'

Secondly: it is true that Calvin stressed the importance of commerce and industry and was more enlightened than Catholic teachers in his attitude to interest. But he laid down severe ethical conditions, often just as constrictive as those of the Catholic church, for economic activity. Free-for-all capitalism was not tolerated.

Thirdly: if, furthermore, a difference did exist between Catholic and Calvinist asceticism in regard to economic activity, this dissimilarity should not be exaggerated. Benedictines, Franciscans and Jesuits come close to Calvinism in this respect.

Fourthly: Weber's observations on the geography of Protestantism and capitalism seem to be wrong. Amsterdam retained its Spanish allegiance longest of all Dutch cities and was long decidedly Catholic; Antwerp has always been Catholic. In England, where the correlation between economic prosperity and Puritanism seems more tangible, motives other than the religious may also have played a substantial part.

Despite these reflections, however, Rachfahl did not reject Weber. In the end he accepted, with certain modifications, the broad conclusion that Protestantism in general and Puritanism in particular had a decisive influence upon economic activity. It was not, however, primarily its distinctive 'spirit of capi-

9

talism' that merited emphasis, but certain other considerations. Rachfahl summarised them in five points:

1. Protestantism permitted the intellect to be devoted to worldly pursuits; in Catholic countries the best brains went into the priesthood.

2. Protestantism brought education to the great masses of the population, thus equipping them better for the economic struggle between nations.

3. By contrast with Catholicism, Protestantism did not encourage the indolence and distaste for labour that are associated with renunciation of the world.

4. Protestantism championed the independence and personal responsibility of the individual; and this had its effect on personal behaviour.

5. Protestantism created a higher type of morality than Catholicism.

Rachfahl sums up: 'in all these respects, Protestantism produced a liberating and stimulating effect upon economic life, but Catholicism a constricting and obstructive one.'

In addition—and Rachfahl declared this aspect to be of even greater moment than those mentioned above—there is the line of demarcation between politics and religion that Protestantism can be seen as having created. In Catholic countries the two were intimately associated. The collaboration between state and church, with the state subordinate to the church, cramped the freedom of personal enterprise. This line of demarcation also made it possible for Protestant countries, especially the Netherlands, to display towards holders of unorthodox views a degree of tolerance that was very important; Rachfahl, like Sombart later, devotes a whole section to the role of 'foreigners' in the economic metamorphosis.

Thus what began as severe criticism of Weber ends by virtual adherence to his views: 'so we must recognise that religious conditions played a considerable part in economic expansion; our inquiries will not, it is true, follow the same direction as Weber's, at least not so exclusively as his; we ought, rather, to seek to analyse the influence of religion in all its aspects, how it sometimes retarded, sometimes encouraged economic development; and we shall find that Protestantism's economic lead derives in essence from the absence in it of those obstructive forces which in Catholicism stood blocking the road towards economic expansion. Among the factors that promoted the latter is, indubitably, the special Reformation concept of a calling and vocation (*Berufsethik*).'[18]

As will shortly appear, Rachfahl did not long remain the sole exponent of this technique of contesting certain fundamental elements of Weber's thesis, only to finish up—after making some further contributions to the problem of why Protestantism was so important—by accepting the basic concept of an indissoluble bond, both worthy and capable of close study, linking religion and economics.

Werner Sombart discussed the matter in his work *Der Bourgeois*, published in 1913, and pressed even more vigorously than Weber the thesis of the contribution of religion to the spirit of capitalism, though he applied it to Catholicism. 'Precapitalism' in the Italian merchant cities was held to be the direct result of the ability of Catholicism to foster a capitalistic outlook; and the financial strength of the Papacy to have materially assisted in the creation of a capitalistic economy and thus, indirectly, a capitalistic outlook.

In the second edition (1916) of his major work *Der moderne Kapitalismus,* Sombart's main preoccupation was with quite a different notion. *Main* must be stressed, for the work is crammed with virtually every conceivable solution to the problems

[18] F. Rachfahl in *Internationale Wochenschrift für Wissenschaft, Kunst und Technik,* Nos. 39—43 (1909). See also Weber's reply, 'Antikritisches zum Geist des Kapitalismus', *Archiv für Sozialwissenschaft,* Vol. XXX (1910). Rachfahl then came back with 'Nochmals Kalvinismus und Kapitalismus', *Internationale Wochenschrift,* Nos. 22—25 (1910), whereupon Weber published an 'Antikritisches Schlusswort' in *Archiv für Sozialwissenschaft,* Vol. XXXI (1910). References to this debate are to be found in the notes to Weber's *Gesammelte Aufsätze.* Weber did not, however, concede any significant point.

11

of economic history—as well as many that are inconceivable. Here it is not religious concepts as such but rather religious persecutions that are crucial. Persecution in some directions, tolerance in others, promoted the dissemination of occupational skills and created classes of people to whom commerce and business came naturally because of their international connections. The Edict of Potsdam, 1685, which opened the Electorate of Brandenburg-Prussia to French adherents of the Reformed church who had been expelled after the revocation of the Edict of Nantes in the same year, is an event of great importance from this point of view.[19]

The scholar who went furthest in criticising Weber—before Robertson at any rate—was Lujo Brentano, in an excursus to his book *Die Anfänge des modernen Kapitalismus,* which appeared in 1916.[20] Like Rachfahl, he scouts the idea of a real 'spirit of capitalism'. By giving the concept a narrow definition, Weber made it fit only Puritan Protestantism, and Benjamin Franklin. Capitalism and the desire to make money and do business existed long before the Reformation, in the Italian cities for instance. When the economic centre of gravity, not because of the Reformation but from other causes, shifted from the Mediterranean to the North Sea, many Catholic merchant families 'moved with it'. Brentano adduces the example of his own family. In the course of the 17th and 18th centuries, members of the Brentano family moved northwards out of Italy and established banking firms and mercantile houses dealing in colonial products in such cities as Amsterdam, Breslau, Mannheim, Augsburg and Frankfurt. These members of the family amassed large—in some cases very large—fortunes. They remained Catholics and were anything but Puritan in their capacity to relish the most elegant pleasures of this world.

[19] As well as *Der Bourgeois* (1913) and *Der moderne Kapitalismus* (2nd Ed. 1916—27), cf. also Sombart's *Die Juden und das Wirtschaftsleben* (1911) and *Luxus und Kapitalismus* (1913).

[20] The work is an elaboration of the approach which he had already put forward in 1913 in his *Münchener Festrede* (Akademi der Wissenschaften).

The Calvinist concept of the 'calling,' Brentano goes on to assert, was by no means peculiar to Calvinism. It is a linguistic error to suppose that an idea or attribute does not exist just because there may not be any adequate expression for it. In any case, the term applied to labour in the Latin translations of the Bible covers 'calling' to the same extent as Luther's *Beruf: vocatio* signifies exactly the same thing as *Beruf* and is used in contexts which show that, even before the Reformation, work and duty were thought to constitute a 'calling' in the sight of God.

Brentano also criticised the idea that the Puritans regarded business activity with any particular favour or were specially imbued with 'the spirit of capitalism'. Of some Puritan writers the opposite seems to be true. In other instances, such as that of Franklin, it is simply a matter of such virtues as industry and thrift and frugality being extolled as they have been extolled in every age and in practically every quarter, religious and non-religious alike. It is not Puritanism that confronts us but the common currency of morality.

Very great importance was attributed by Brentano to Roman law and its attitude to business conduct. It is wrong, he says, to view canonical law as the one applicable to practical life. The rules of Roman law were enforced in business activity and other practical affairs independently of the Catholic and later the Protestant faith: 'The spirit of capitalism arose with trade, whose essence is the struggle for the highest possible profit. Its diffusion went hand in hand with the growth of trade.'[21] What was most significant was the revival and extension of the supremacy of Roman law. This law had its origins in the stoic philosophy. The stoics' line of thought followed concepts of natural law. Complete harmony exists between nature and reason, between the natural and the existing order. From this, says Brentano, it was not a long step to a spirit of capitalism in the sense that what was done by the 'best', the most successful, was right. These ideas were contrary to the teaching of the

[21] *Anfänge des modernen Kapitalismus*, p. 154.

13

Catholic church: 'But since it was evident that economic activity could not be pursued in accordance with Christ's message without losing ground in economic respects, people chose as their guide to conduct, not what was taught by the church, but what was prescribed by worldly law for worldly situations.' [22]

Nevertheless, Brentano did not completely reject Weber. It can by no means be denied, he declares, that wherever there already existed a well-developed capitalism, the Puritan doctrine of grace gave the spirit of capitalism a religious inspiration and force that lent a powerful impulse to its further diffusion.

The English historian, William Ashley, whose work was quite independent of Weber's, primarily emphasised the change which the emergence of Calvinism seems to have wrought in the attitude towards usury. He found in this an explanation of that disparity in economic energy as between Calvinists and Lutherans which Weber postulated. Luther never managed to break with the canonical view: 'The hatred of usury was so ingrained in the people that a peasant's son like Luther could hardly be free from it; and enthusiasm for moral reform, which was the main cause of the new religious movement, reverted naturally to earlier and severe standards.' [23] In Melanchthon, however, there are signs of a more enlightened outlook, and the open break with the old conception of usury is made by Calvin. The latter's disavowal, in 1545, of the view that the exaction of interest was sinful came to be regarded by later generations as a defence of virtually any kind of usury. The opportunity of increasing one's capital by investment was thus presented. An important component of a 'capitalistic' system had gained acceptance. The turning point had been reached.

Ashley did not, however, believe that the effect produced on economic evolution by the new religious ideas was deliberate;

[22] *Ibid.*, p. 157.
[23] W. Ashley, *Introduction to English Economic History and Theory* (1st Ed. 1888—93), 4th Ed. (1906), Vol. I, Part II, p. 456. See in general the chapter entitled 'The Canonist Doctrine'.

that Calvinism, for instance, *intended* to promote a new economic ideology. On the contrary, he stressed the lack of interest in such problems among religious leaders. The impact upon economic thought and action was a secondary one.

From this position it is not a long step to that adopted by R. H. Tawney.[24] He begins by reversing the approach to the original problem. He underlines, though less heavily than Weber and Ashley, the importance of Calvinism; and he emphasises, more strongly than Weber, the difference between Calvin and Luther. But he sees nascent capitalism as the prime factor. It is this which conditions Calvinism's attitude to enterprise and the accumulation of wealth, not *vice versa*. Early Calvinism and the first Puritan movements in England rapidly reinforced the moralistic, Old Testament view of business life and enterprise. Geographical discoveries, new techniques, and the operations of the great mercantile houses of Augsburg, Lisbon and Antwerp had long before this combined to produce, independently of religious conceptions, the economic expansion of the 16th and early 17th centuries for which the ground had been prepared in Italy, Spain and Portugal. The spirit of capitalism, says Tawney, is as old as history. 'If capitalism means the direction of industry by owners of capital for their own pecuniary gain, and the social relations which establish themselves between them and the wage-earning proletariat whom they control, then capitalism had existed on a grand scale both in medieval Italy and in medieval Flanders. If by the capitalist spirit is meant the temper which is prepared to sacrifice all moral scruples to the pursuit of profit, it had been only too familiar to the saints and sages of the Middle Ages.' [25] It was Catholic Portugal and Catholic Spain that were the great conquerors; it was predominantly Catholic cities that were the chief commercial capitals of Europe; it was Catholic bankers who were the leading financiers.

[24] R. H. Tawney, *Religion and the Rise of Capitalism* (1926).
[25] *Ibid.*, p. 84.

However, in step with the economic transformation of the 16th and 17th centuries, the religious outlook underwent a change as well. It is in the Puritan sects that this change is principally discernible. Calvinism, and Puritanism especially, took on a 'capitalistic' flavour, through their effect upon the opinions of the mass of the people, even if not in the minds of the great exponents of doctrine. This new attitude cleared the way for a more forcible expansion of capitalism than would otherwise have been possible. Tawney dwells particularly upon the contribution made to this development by the conception of the 'calling'. Thus his approach to the problem comes, in the end, to view Calvinism and Puritanism as the decisive factors. 'The idea of economic progress as an end to be consciously sought, while ever receding, had been unfamiliar to most earlier generations of Englishmen, in which the theme of moralists had been the danger of unbridled cupidity, and the main aim of public policy had been the stability of traditional relationships. It found a new sanction in the identification of labour and enterprise with the service of God. The magnificent energy which changed in a century the face of material civilization was to draw nourishment from that temper.' [26] Such a transformation occurred in all Calvinist countries: in Holland, in Scotland, in America, and indeed, in Geneva itself. Calvinism had begun as the doctrine of religious collectivism and discipline, 'the very soul of authoritarian regimentation.' It ended 'by being the vehicle of an almost Utilitarian individualism.' [27]

Tawney's precursory criticisms of Weber were complemented by those of H. M. Robertson,[28] these being based mainly on chronological grounds. Firstly, says Robertson, capitalism and what may be termed the capitalistic spirit existed long before the ideas of the Reformation began to assert themselves. Like Sombart, he dwells upon such phenomena as the Italian mer-

[26] *Ibid.*, p. 249. [27] *Ibid.*, p. 227.
[28] H. M. Robertson, *Aspects of the Rise of Economic Individualism. A Criticism of Max Weber and his School* (1933).

16

chant cities. Secondly, there were tendencies in Catholicism too that may be viewed as having fostered a capitalistic spirit, e.g., the energy of the Jesuits, which extended to business as well as religion, and the thrift of the Franciscans. Moreover, several Catholic writers displayed a far greater understanding of interest than did Luther or even Calvin, and the nonconformist sects were violently censorious of high rates of interest. More than half of Robertson's book is devoted to such questions as pre-Reformation capitalism, the Renaissance state, the influence of the Jesuits and the general approach of Catholicism to economic affairs.

Robertson also levels criticism at Weber's and Tawney's concept of the 'calling'. Ranging himself alongside Brentano, he rejects in no uncertain terms the idea that through Calvinism and the sects the 'calling' attained both spiritual and worldly significance, and that the religious call thus became synonymous with everyday work, with the vocation in life—*der Beruf*. By Calvin, as by French-speaking writers generally, it is called *office,* a word which then, as well as earlier and later, denoted in the Latin languages (Latin and Italian *officio*, French *office,* Spanish *oficio*) not only 'vocation' in the everyday sense of 'employment' but also the religious 'calling,' 'worship'. The idea of a connection between daily, worldly duty and the service of God was, writes Robertson, one that had long been present in Catholicism; and he cites a number of writings, chiefly by Jesuit authors, all of which assert the same idea: God grants his grace to us for that which we do for our own temporal welfare, if it is done for the love of God. Man may be a soldier, judge or businessman, but at the same time he is a Christian too. He can serve the same Master in all these various ways, and he can at one and the same time labour fruitfully for God, for Humanity and for himself.[29]

If there was any change of outlook on economic activity after the Reformation, then, Robertson maintains, it occurred during

[29] *Ibid.,* Chap. I, *passim.*

the second half of the 17th century. It is then that industry, thrift and labour as a Godly duty seem to be more heavily emphasised than before. But this increase of emphasis was just as marked in Catholic as in Protestant countries: '. . . they spread both amongst Protestants and Catholics. It would appear that this is in itself enough to prove that the problem has been viewed through the wrong end of the telescope—to show that the chief relation between the rise of the capitalistic spirit and the Protestant Ethic is the reverse of what Weber has indicated. The Protestant Ethic changed as a result of the influence of a rising capitalistically-minded middle class. The churches of the Calvinists and the Puritans did not always bear the same witness as regards the duties of the man of business. A changing emphasis, reflecting a changing spirit of the age, transformed a doctrine outwardly uniform. From being a hindrance to enterprise it became a spur.' [30] This, it is evident, is not far removed from Tawney and his 'later' Puritanism.

Robertson invokes the geographical discoveries to explain the fact that the capitalism of the new age made its first appearance in such Protestant countries as England and the Netherlands. They caused the economic centres of the world to shift westwards away from Italy. Spain, however, was prevented from enjoying the fruits of this change because of its policy of regulation, which was inimical to trade. That the most capitalistic countries, and the merchant and similar classes within them especially, were Protestant, Robertson ascribes to an easier spread of new ideas amongst trading nations and peoples. At the time when Florence, Genoa, Venice and other Italian cities were deeply involved in the development of commerce in the Mediterranean region, they were also the centres of a capitalistic and individualistic movement of which the Renaissance was one aspect. It seems probable that the growth of trade across the Atlantic and Indian Oceans was a primary cause of the rise of economic individualism in western Europe during the

[30] *Ibid.*, pp. 31—32.

18

16th and 17th centuries: 'The spirit of capitalism is not the creator but the creation of the class of businessmen.' [31]

In certain respects Robertson was palpably indebted to Sombart. The heavy emphasis on the deviation of pre-Reformation Catholicism into a more 'capitalistic' course, and on the comparability of the Jesuits and other orders with the reformatory movements in regard to their impact upon economic life—or at any rate upon views about it: these correspond closely with Sombart's ideas. On this latter point Robertson received an immediate rejoinder from a Jesuit, James Brodrick. In a work entitled *The Economic Morals of the Jesuits, an Answer to Dr. H. M. Robertson* (1934), he asserted that Robertson's analysis of the doctrines of the Jesuits was utterly incorrect. He maintained that to attribute to them doctrines on economic matters similar to those ascribed by Weber to Calvinism and the nonconformist sects was a grave misinterpretation. Usury, diligence, the concept of the 'calling': none of these was allowed a free rein by the Jesuits.

Robertson's stress on the great significance of the geographical discoveries and the new trade routes did not go unsupported. In the same year as Robertson published his work, the Catholic author Fanfani put forward almost exactly the same theories about economic expansion and the reorientation of trade.[32] In Fanfani's view, religion was of quite subordinate importance. The spirit of capitalism is foreign to every kind of religion. To the extent that Protestantism had any effect, it did not arise from this form of religion making work into a 'calling' in the sense intended by Weber, but from the fact that in practice it divorced labour from religious life and thereby released economic activity from the inhibitions of religion.

The idea that changes requisite to the rise of capitalism occurred independently of the Reformation had been suggested by Cunningham a couple of years before the publication of

[31] *Ibid.*, p. 177.
[32] A. Fanfani, *Catholicism, Protestantism and Capitalism* (1935; English translation, 1936).

19

Weber's work. He considered that the pre-conditions for what he calls the 'intervention of capitalism' were laid down during the 15th and 16th centuries; they arose from the disintegration, under the impact of the forces that made for the creation of new national states hostile to the papal power, of the social system built up by Catholicism. In this way rivalry was created between peoples, and the western community was deprived of its static, medieval impress. Secularisation, not religion, stands out as the vital factor. Calvin and Calvinism are not mentioned at all.[33]

This was Cunningham before Weber. Ten years later, under the influence of Weber and his disciple Troeltsch, some different ideas made their appearance. In his *Christianity and Economic Science,* Cunningham quotes Presbyterian Scotland as the outstanding example of Calvinism's capacity to impel people to economic activity and 'capitalism'. 'Not till it spread to Scotland did Calvinism achieve its full development ... and it is in Scotland that we can best see the influence of Calvinism on national life.'[34] The ideas of the Presbyterians, he says, caused great interest to be devoted in Scotland to the provision of work for the unemployed, in effect to the elimination of unemployment, and to setting children to work early, so that they might learn habits of diligence and evade the pitfalls of idleness. 'The seventeenth century Presbyterian took a stern view of the discipline which was good for children, so that they might be kept from forming habits of idleness and form drifting into evil of every kind.'[35] 'Calvinism,' he continues, 'is a form of Christianity which gave its sanction to the free exersice of the commercial spirit and to the capitalist organisation of industry.'[36]

[33] W. Cunningham, *An Essay on Western Civilization in its Economic Aspects,* Vol. II (1904), *passim.*

[34] W. Cunningham, *Christianity and Economic Science* (1914), p. 66.

[35] *Ibid.,* p. 68.

[36] *Ibid.,* pp. 69—70. See also E. Troeltsch, *Die Sociallehren der christlichen Kirchen und Gruppen* (1912). (English translation: *The Social Teachings of the Christian Churches,* 2 vols. 1931.) In all essentials Troeltsch's ideas link up with Weber's on the viewpoints considered here. The main difference can be said to be that Troeltsch was more interested

Cunningham does not, however, offer any further proof; he simply declares that it is superfluous after Weber's work. Scotland is conclusive proof that it is within Christianity itself, through Calvinism, that the necessary transformation occurs—that, in other words, Sombart's theory of the contribution of the Jews is erroneous.

Apart from Fanfani, the most important examination of Weber's thesis from the Catholic viewpoint is that made by Professor J. B. Kraus, of the Catholic university of Tokio.[37]

Professor Kraus, a Jesuit, heavily underlines the divergence, also noted by Weber at one point, between original Calvinist thought and the 'capitalistic' outlook on life. The rudimentary beginnings of such an attitude, originally to be found in Calvinism, were reinforced by the pressure of economic reality. Kraus' kinship with Tawney on this point is manifest. It is possible, he believes further, to speak of an interaction of forces between economics and religion of such a nature that a purely 'materialistic' and a purely 'idealistic' approach are both unrealistic. In other words, by saying that each idea is rubbish on its own but that there is a morsel of the soundest commonsense in both, Kraus contrives to make a compromise: 'the old phrase *in medio stat virtus* may be thought the most sensible solution here too,'[38] he sums up sapiently.

The difference thought by Weber to exist on the usury question between the traditionalist Luther and the more favourably disposed Calvin is not considered by Kraus—here again on the same line as Tawney—to be of much worth. Calvin and his immediate followers were in reality bound by tradition almost as much as Luther. It is only under the pressure of economic progress that some adaptation occurs: as, for instance, with the

in the teachings themselves, in religious views as such, whilst Weber's interest was almost wholly in the practical importance of religion for economic and social life.

[37] J. B. Kraus, *Scholastik, Puritanismus und Kapitalismus. Eine vergleichende dogmengeschichtliche Übergangsstudie* (1930).

[38] *Ibid.*, p. 292.

English Puritans—who were essentially as good schoolmen as the schoolmen themselves. Adjustment is forced upon them, and this afterwards leads to a capitalistically coloured ideology. The evolution of the English economy was certainly not produced by religious circumstances but by general economic conditions, 'but the development was able to proceed so freely and uninhibitedly thanks to the demolition of old hindrances and limitations, a demolition which went hand in hand with the religious emancipation.'[39] Puritanism thus gradually becomes a motivating force as the economic trend continues. Kinship with Tawney is discernible here too.

When writing of 'the role of foreigners,' Sombart represented the impact of religion upon economic development as a wholly indirect relationship, in which religious concepts as such are of no importance to economic actions. This is a clearly anti-Weber line of thought. T. S. Ashton reveals a similar approach, although in quite a different context; his observations are, moreover, confined solely to Great Britain. Why were there so many Nonconformists amongst the entrepreneurs of the Industrial Revolution? The explanation of the economic energy and achievements of these Dissenters was not their religious attachment in itself (although there may be something in this idea, Ashton adds, though without adducing any proof) but the higher education, often with a marked leaning towards the natural sciences, provided at the Scottish universities and the dissenting academies.[40]

Oddly enough, Weber's theories have attracted very little attention in the Netherlands, where they should have found particular confirmation. As far as I know, his ideas only came into fashion there in the 1930s, when they were expounded in

[39] *Ibid.,* p. 307.

[40] T. S. Ashton, *The Industrial Revolution* (1948), pp. 17 ff. See also his *Iron and Steel in the Industrial Revolution* (1924, 2nd ed. 1951) esp. Chap. IV, where he discusses the religion of the Quakers as an explanation of their achievements. See also below, pp. 122—5.

an academic treatise by W. F. van Gunsteren.[41] It is interesting, however, that nowhere—in a work of about 300 pages—does van Gunsteren make any effort to prove a correlation between religious belief and economic progress in the Netherlands. In the main, he does not attempt to study the facts but confines himself to a general exposition, in the spirit of Weber, of Protestant writings, especially those of the Reformed religion. In a brief paper three years earlier, Ernst Bein had discussed the economic views of the Dutch Reformed Church, but without finding any support at all for Weber's theories.[42]

In 1940 a Dane, Wolmer Clemmensen, published a study of the influence of religious doctrines on economic ethics in Denmark.[43] Clemmensen, too, restricts himself to a study of the literature, and tries to trace in it the spirit of capitalism and the evolution of the ethic of enterprise in Denmark. Since Denmark was overwhelmingly Lutheran, he does not suppose that he can expect very much—i.e., he has learnt from Weber that there ought not to be much for him to expect. In Denmark the Lutheran state church held all other movements at bay: 'thus religious systems such as Calvinism, Puritanism and Judaism, so important to the capitalist ethic, were denied entry.'[44] The later 'state Pietism' admittedly broke with the Lutheran tradition in a number of respects, but where economic ethics were concerned they both followed the same line: 'There consequently arose a special Lutheran-Pietistic mode of life that strengthened the inhibition, engendered by the economic development of the country, against the emerging capitalist ethic in the rigorous form that it took in the countries specifically affected by Calvinistic Puritanism.'[45]

Though prudently emphasising that the importance of the

[41] W. F. Van Gunsteren, *Kalvinismus und Kapitalismus* (1934).

[42] E. Bein, 'Die Wirtschaftsethik der calvinistischen Kirche der Niederlande, 1565—1650'. *Niederlandsch Archief voor Kerkegeschiedenis* (1931), Vol. XXIV, pp. 81—156.

[43] W. Clemmensen, *De Religiöse Systemers Indflydelse paa de erhvervsetiske Princippers Udvikling i Danmark* (1940).

[44] *Ibid.*, p. 280.   [45] *Ibid.*, p. 280.

Lutheran-Pietist influence must not be exaggerated, Clemmensen considers that its strength was nevertheless sufficient to corroborate indirectly the theses of Weber and Sombart concerning the significance of Puritanism and Judaism in the evolution and ethic of capitalism. Therefore, he continues, the inquiry has disclosed that 'only in its Calvinist-Puritan form can the Reformation have offered an effective foundation for the spirit of capitalism.'[46] But Clemmensen also asserts that religious concepts cannot be proved to have had any influence upon economic trends. Indeed, Danish experience shows that they did not. At which stage confusion is confounded and tedium has arrived.

On one point Clemmensen is clearly—though from all the indications not consciously—an anti-Weberian. According to Weber, it was in Franklin that the capitalist ethic reached full maturity and by the captains of industry that it was practised in full measure. But Clemmensen stresses the disappearance of the Puritan ethic with modern industrial capitalism. By way of the 'survival of the fittest,' the capitalist ethic entered upon an immoral period: the consequence was a 'morality of success,' in which anything was permitted as long as the letter of the law was kept. In brief, Clemmensen is critical of free competition and modern industrial capitalism, and is anxious to set a limit to the influence of religion at the point where economic evolution takes a turn which he views unsympathetically.

4. THE PROBLEM

From this survey of the controversy[47] it is apparent that even writers who have criticised Weber's theories at point after point

[46] *Ibid.*, p. 281.

[47] The writers who have been mentioned in the foregoing section represent the controversy simply so far as its central questions are concerned. In general, on Christianity and social life, on Puritanism, etc., an array of works has been published, to all of which it is impossible to refer in this present context. Some will be cited below. Others characteristic of

24

have nevertheless been kind enough to finish up by finding a certain plausibility in them. Agreed that Weber exaggerated, that his generalisations tend to be sweeping, that he ignored factors other than Protestantism, that the relationship between Protestantism and economic progress is not so direct or so immediate as Weber would have it. And yet in the end it is admitted that the basic premises for Weber's assertions hold good. There was a clear connection between Protestantism and economic progress. Even the more critical writers such as Robertson, after attacking the Weberian correlation on various grounds, have turned the penny over and announced the relationship to be of the opposite nature: it was economic activity that engendered religious change, not religion that transformed economic life. Halfway between Weber and this inversion of Weber stand those who, like Tawney and Kraus, speak in highly general terms of the interplay between economic and religious changes, of the ability of economics to transform religious doctrine and of the transformed religious doctrine's capacity to 'deepen' and 'nurture' the spirit of capitalism in return. Such writers, disposed to compromise, evidently believe that false concepts can be made into perfectly sensible ones simply by taking little bits of each and glueing them together into a 'between-the-two' or 'as-well-as' joinery of totally opposed notions.

The starting point of the argument that follows is different from that of the writers discussed above in that it does not take the form of a quest for explanations, wholly or partly new, of the connection between Protestantism and economic progress. Admittedly this book too will consider such questions as: What was the attitude of Protestantism, and Puritanism in particular, to wealth and capitalism? Did such a connection or affinity exist between Puritanism and the 'spirit of capitalism' that the

this body of writing include V. A. Demant, *Religion and the Decline of Capitalism* (1952), D. L. Munby, *Christianity and Economic Problems* (1956), J. Stamp, *The Christian Ethic as an Economic Factor* (1926), and A. D. Lindsay, *Christianity and Economics* (1930).

latter may be regarded as having found its incarnation in Benjamin Franklin and the American captains of industry? What part was played by diligence, thrift and free interest rates in the evolution of capitalism?

But the object of this inquiry is not to find an explanation of the connection between Protestantism and economic progress. The question posed instead is *whether* such a connection existed at all, *whether* the problem deliberated upon by Weber and his disciples, equally with his bitterest critics, is properly framed. Did such a clear correlation exist between Protestantism and economic progress that there is any reason to inquire into cause and effect at all?

CHAPTER II

The Spirit of Puritanism and

the Spirit of Capitalism

1. THE PURITAN FATHERS

That Luther and his successors were but little interested in economic questions even Weber recognised. The chief significance of Lutheranism outside the immediate religious situation lay on the political plane, in the replacement of the Roman church by state churches and the resultant addition to the weapons of power and propaganda in the hands of the new principalities. It is indisputable too that the new organisational forms, the more virile national states incorporating kingship by Divine Right (a principle never fully recognised in Catholicism), affected economic life; and, conversely, that they owed some part of their origin to economic changes. But this has nothing to do with Weber's thesis.

In their purely political aspect, the Calvinistic Reformed church creeds differed from the Lutheran Protestant. They did not usually make compacts with governmental and princely powers, but sought in their relations with them the same freedom in religious matters as they enjoyed *vis-à-vis* the Holy See. To quite a large extent they thus came to represent and create opposition, and to appeal with particular force to opposition factions such as the 'free merchant cities' and other corporative entities struggling for greater economic, social and political freedom of movement. On this account economic problems presented themselves more urgently to the Free Church fathers than to

Catholicism and Lutheranism. Calvin, Baxter, Wesley, Fox and Penn all touched upon such problems in their sermons and writings.[1]

Thus far we can admit Weber to be right. But the common, pervading tone of their pronouncements upon economic matters is one, not of exhortation and encouragement, but of acquiescence, conceded with varying degrees of readiness and sometimes with manifest reluctance, in economic activity. Such activity is not depicted as being in itself pleasing in the sight of God. It is merely stated that it *need* not be abhorrent if pursued in the right spirit. It does not open the gates of Heaven. But neither, at its best, does it block the road to them. As writers such as Ashley and Kraus have stressed and as even Weber half-heartedly acknowledged on one occasion, there is no question of these sects bringing in a new economic ideology any more than did the original Calvinism. The prophets of the Reformed and Free Churches were not out to give instructions in economics. But to satisfy the classes that these movements were primarily seeking to win over, it was necessary to take up some position on the subject of economic activity. In determining that position, however, the problems of capitalism had the least say of all.

It was some time before Calvin was ready to deny that the

[1] On Lutheranism and the political environment, see, e.g. A. Ross, *Why Democracy* (1952), p. 16 ff., and E. Barker, *Principles of Political and Social Theory* (1951), pp. 13 ff., esp. p. 15. On the Reformed church and state power, see, in addition to the Free church fathers cited in the text, K. S. Latourette, *A History of Christianity* (1953), p. 774 ff. The analysis in the following pages of Puritan teachings and economic behaviour draws upon W. J. Warner, *The Wesleyan Movement in the Industrial Revolution* (1930) esp. pp. 136—216, 1. Grubb, *Quakerism and Industry before 1800* (1930) esp. pp. 36—40, together with accounts in the already quoted works of Tawney, Robertson, Kraus and Broderick; but above all upon *The Works of the Rev. John Wesley*, vols. 10—11 (ed. 1820—21), *The Journal of George Fox*, I—II (ed. 1891), esp. II, p. 493, W. Penn, *A Brief Account of the Rise and Progress of the People called Quakers* (ed. 1748), R. Baxter, *A Christian Directory, or a Summ of Practical Theologie and Cases of Conscience* (1673, select passages, ed. J. Tawney, 1925), J. Bunyan, *The Life and Death of Mr. Badman* (1680) and *Pilgrim's Progress* (1673).

exaction of interest was wicked, and he did so with much hesitancy. George Fox enveloped his recognition of economic prosperity as being tolerable to religion with such an array of moral homilies on the proper treatment of employees, on the setting of 'just' prices and on honourable dealings with business partners that it leaves a clear impression of doubt and distaste. And when John Wesley proclaimed his *dictum,* quoted by Weber, that 'religion must necessarily produce both industry and frugality, and these cannot but produce riches',[2] the context was rather the reverse of that implied by Weber. Wesley is not applauding riches as such. But since industry is a virtue, since frugality is a virtue, and since it is from the virtues that wealth arises, then wealth and success in trade or industry cannot possibly be wicked of themselves, even if their results were often an iniquitous mode of life and the forsaking of righteous Christian principles. Wealth results from two virtues pleasing to our Lord and therefore—but only therefore, and under definite conditions—becomes worthy of approbation.

Just as St. Paul made Christianity more acceptable to the Hellenic world of his day by incorporating in it elements of Greek philosophy, and just as missionaries of the Catholic church in northern Europe smoothed the path for the conversion of the Vikings and other heathens by blurring as far as possible the distinctions between the old gods and the new God, so did certain leaders of the Free Church movement, confronted with the task of winning over merchants and other business men, find themselves having to adopt as sympathetic a position as possible towards wealth and economic activity. They let it be understood—and under the influence of the environment presumably believed themselves to be right—that in certain defined conditions the rich man had at least the same chance as the camel.

But from acquiescence to positive impulse is a long step. A 'spirit of capitalism' is not generated merely by allowing business men to enter the Kingdom of Heaven on the same terms

[2] Quoted *Protestant Ethic,* p. 175.

as other groups. George Fox did not bring economic success to his Quakers. But it is possible that his broad demand for freedom from governmental coercion in religious matters was particularly attractive to groups already eager for freedom in economic affairs and for the emancipation of trade and industry. The alliance of the Anglican church with landowners and the landed interest made it natural that the opposition to these interests, represented by merchants, industrialists and artisans, should range itself with elements opposed to patronage and the Established church. Thus it was that, subject to explicitly defined reservations, the force of circumstances engendered in these circles some degree of indulgence towards economic success, as a kind of appendix—though often not a very bulky one—to the main exposition of faith.

Calvin's view of the concept of profit is particularly interesting. God does not forbid profit altogether, he declared in delivering his celebrated verdict on the usury problem: 'For how could this be possible? It would compel us to cease all commerce; it would be clearly unlawful for people to conduct business with each other in the manner they now do.' But there are definite limits. God forbids that profit 'which is secured by him who purchases his goods without bearing any risk, and likewise frowns on him who heeds not whether he injures his neighbour, but thinks only to enrich himself (*mais il se veut enricher*).'[3] When business transactions and interest charges transgress the bounds set by the 'just price,' the level of profit corresponding to the time and trouble incurred, and the ordinary need for a livelihood, when the motive of self-enrichment appears, then there is sin. The environment in which Calvin lived, like his upbringing, made it natural and inevitable that he should make allowance for 'sociological' factors side by side with theological considerations, for 'facts as well as words'. But in this he does not differ from Augustine or

[3] Quoted H. Hauser, *Les Débuts du Capitalisme* (1927), p. 73. See further Calvin's *Institution de la religion chrétienne*. (New edition published by the Société Calviniste de France, 1955.)

Thomas Aquinas. They, too, saw that the 'world outside' was otherwise constituted and that practical life demanded exceptions to the rules. The difference consists in the fact that Calvin's environment was one of business and a money economy, whilst that of the early fathers was pastoral and agricultural. But the anti-capitalist theme, the view that riches and the lust for them were wicked, was common to all three. Wealth as an end in itself was odious.

In fact, there is a whole host of Free Church fathers in whom can be found, exactly as in Calvin, the most contradictory attitudes to economic activity. One hand confers blessings: many religious leaders undoubtedly favoured diligence, thrift and individual freedom in economic as in political affairs. But the other heaps anathemas: in place of governmental regulation, business men were confronted with stern moralistic injunctions on such matters as pricing policy, interest rates and the like. The demands of both Fox and Wesley for the 'just price' were so uncompromising as to bear comparison with canonical law. The 'righteous' use of riches, like the idea of 'trusteeship,' when developed to such a degree that inheritance above a certain maximum was considered repugnant, was equally inhibitory.

What was preached was in truth no free-for-all capitalism of the kind that came to hold sway over the industrialising nations in the later 18th and the 19th centuries, but the business activity of a world of small traders and handicrafts, hedged around with moralistic precepts and dogmas. It is for this reason that Wellman J. Warner, who sought to apply Weber's principles to a study of Wesleyanism and the Industrial Revolution,[4] is again and again forced explicitly or implicitly to admit weaknesses in the argument. Wesley's economic reflections were in many respects conditioned by the epoch of economic organisation which was just then passing away. They did not fit the new forms of industrial life. The important elements in 'capitalism' constituted by speculation and the exploitation

[4] W. J. Warner, *op. cit.*

of monopoly, both before and during the Industrial Revolution, were condemned by Methodists and Quakers alike.

More important than this, however, is the fact that the inculcation of virtues that were thought to lead to wealth went hand in hand with hostility towards wealth as such and fear of its demoralising influence. If success in business signalised the favour of the Almighty, so did it at the same time place the successful in peril of a swift fall from His grace. Even though the rich are not necessarily to be regarded as children of wickedness, wrote Wesley, riches are dangerous nevertheless. 'It is absolutely impossible, unless by that Power to which all things are possible, that a rich man should be a Christian.' Riches lead people to 'love of the world, desire of pleasure, of ease, of getting money.'[5] Riches, moreover, create a sense of cleavage between man and man; they stand in the way of equality. From the socio-economic point of view, moreover, riches cause the rich to procure the production of luxuries, while the poor go short of necessities. This clearly conflicts with Tawney's assertion that the Puritans saw in riches 'not an object for suspicion ... but the blessing which rewards the triumph of energy and will.'[6]

From the same source come two further propositions which, whatever else they may be, cannot in reason be called 'capitalistic'—one is the condemnation of inheritance (over and above what is necessary for the sustenance of the survivors); and the second, the prohibition on the conduct of business with money other than one's own in excess of full collateral available in existing goods: one must 'owe no man anything'. On any credible definition, 'capitalism' before or after the Industrial Revolution implies mobilisation of capital and the large-scale use of credit; and this granting of credit, both by its very nature and as all experience confirms, is largely a gamble upon the success of the borrower, not a loan or ad-

[5] Wesley, *Works.*
[6] *Religion and the Rise of Capitalism,* p. 231.

32

vance furnished upon full security in goods already in existence.[7]

The most exhaustive of his homilies on economic matters Wesley called *The Danger of Riches* and *The Danger of Increasing Riches*. The former he declared to be his first real attempt to analyse the problem posed in the title. He states, moreover, that he has never read any searching study of the subject. The theme is a verse from St. Paul's First Epistle to Timothy, VI. 9: 'But they that will be rich fall into temptation and a snare, and into many foolish and hurtful lusts, which drown men in destruction and perdition.' How incalculable are the unhappy consequences of mankind's failure to apprehend or thoroughly reflect upon this great truth, exclaims Wesley. Many have perhaps been aware of it. But men have sought to reinterpret it, to make it apply only to the amassing of riches at any cost, only to the fortune wrongfully gained. But that cannot be all that it means. If that were so, it could just as well have been omitted from the Bible: 'This is so far from being the whole meaning of the text, that it is no part of its meaning ... The Apostle does not here speak of gaining riches unjustly, but of quite another thing: his words are to be taken in their plain obvious sense, without any restriction or qualification whatsoever.' It means quite simply 'all those who want to be rich.'[8]

Do we not see all around us, Wesley continues, that the rich, instead of being the happiest, are the unhappiest, the most wretched, of mortals?

'You know that in seeking happiness from riches, you are only striving to drink out of empty cups. And let them be painted and gilded ever so finely, they are empty still.'

And:

'O, ye Methodists, hear the word of the Lord! ... who has

[7] For definitions of Capitalism see, e.g. J. Schumpeter, *Business Cycles. A Theoretical, Historical and Statistical Analysis of the Capitalist Process* (2 vols., 1929). Vol. I, p. 233 ff.

[8] Wesley, *op. cit.*

believed our report? I fear: not many rich. I fear there is need to apply to some of you those terrible words of the Apostle. And so Wesley quotes:

"Go to now, ye rich men! Weep and howl for the miseries which shall come upon you. Your gold and silver are cankered, and the rust of them shall witness against you, and shall eat your flesh, as it were fire." [9]

'I have told you,' says Wesley, after these outbursts which, in all reason, testify to anything but a 'spirit of capitalism' (he has picked out the most 'anti-capitalistic' passage in the Bible), that you must work and save. But may you then not become rich? No, you shall give away what you have earned and saved, give it to the poor: 'Having gained, in a right sense, all you can, and saved all you can; in spite of nature and custom and worldly prudence, give all you can.' But do not, as the Jews do, give only a tenth, nor like the Pharisees only a fifth, of your possessions: 'I dare not advise you to give half of what you have, nor three quarters, but all.' [10]

An important theme in the economic teachings of Quaker preachers was that of moderation in business life. Men should not strive to build their businesses to an enormous size, but should confine themselves within the bounds set by their individual capacities. This rule was decreed by Benjamin Lindley, for example, just as strictly as the demand for the just price.[11] In 1680, Stephen Crisp warned his fellow-believers in most emphatic terms against focusing too much of their interest upon worldly affairs—including business and enterprise. Diligence and the observance of duty are important, it is true. But they must not be taken too far. The risk of turning diligence into slavery must be avoided. For this may cause the longing for riches to become 'daily more and more, till a man comes in time to have the increase or decrease of these things to be the objects of his joy or sorrow, and then he is miserable.' [12]

[9] *Ibid.* [10] *Ibid.* [11] See Grubb, *op. cit.,* p. 36 ff. [12] Quoted *ibid.,* p. 37.

The Quaker fathers, sums up Isabel Grubb, had no ambition to press business activity, as Tawney claimed, 'as far as it will go.' She continues: 'Puritanism has been charged with being an important factor in the creation of the modern capitalistic spirit: but if that means that the accumulation of wealth is to be regarded as a good in itself, then the Friends have combated such an opinion.'[13] She unhesitatingly rejects assertions to the effect that the Quaker families were characterised by special competence in business matters and that this was fostered by their religion: 'I have not found any evidence in support of this statement, but some to the contrary.'[14]

Quaker teachings, like those of the Methodists, strongly deprecated extensive credit operations. Credit was permissible where there was collateral in the form of goods. But lending and borrowing for speculative purposes were condemned. William Penn asserted this with no less vigour than others; and at the same time he preached, echoing the writers quoted above, the importance of realising 'when one had sufficient.'[15] A man might strive for a tolerable livelihood, but not for riches. To labour in order to amass a large fortune is to be enslaved. The love of money is conjoined with the love of luxury and—even more harshly castigated by Penn—the love of gold for its own sake, the mad hunger of the miser.

Weber adduces as one of the most telling proofs of his theses the Puritan, Richard Baxter, and his work *A Christian Directory or a Summ of Practical Theologie and Cases of Conscience.* This work, which was published in 1673, Tawney also regards as a *Summa Theologica* and *Summa Moralis* of Puritanism in one.[16] Baxter, declares Weber, impressed upon the reader's mind how pernicious are extravagance and indolence. The call to 'work while the day is with us' was thus elevated to a key position. For a man to fail to employ fruitfully the time given

[13] *Ibid.*

[14] *Ibid.,* p. 36 *n*. See also p. 93 ff.

[15] W. Penn, *A Brief Account of the Rise and Progress of the People called Quakers* (ed. 1748).

[16] *Religion and the Rise of Capitalism,* p. 220.

35

to him is the greatest and in principle the most grievous of all sins. The saying of St. Paul, Weber goes on, that he who will not work, neither shall he eat, is applied by Baxter *'bedingungslos und für jedermann'*, unconditionally and to every man. Want of eagerness to toil is a symptom that God's mercy is withheld. It did not apparently disturb Weber that such notions, even according to the comparisons he himself makes, had been preached ever since at least St. Paul's day, and that Thomas Aquinas had ardently fought the same battle. In the eyes of the latter, he explains, work was only *a naturali ratione,* an activity necessary to sustain life. Not until the Puritans came on the scene did it become a 'call,' a duty before the Lord.[17]

It seems scarcely necessary to point out how far-fetched such imaginings are. Neither in St. Paul nor in Baxter do the texts which Weber is interpreting form coherent chains of reasoning with logically connected ideas from which can be deduced a clear diagnosis of the specific problems such as are being considered. The source material, in both cases, consists of a few sentences, statements made on isolated occasions and devoid of mutual relation, often clearly contradictory and not infrequently framed with such oracular sophistry that it is impossible for the reader of a later age to determine with certainty the 'intrinsic meaning', much less to draw delicate inferences of the type propounded by Weber. Indeed, the writers themselves often never intended to take up any clear position. They found it difficult to reconcile different passages of the Bible with the diverse declarations of earlier church fathers; and when asked to elucidate for the benefit of the community at large which rule was applicable, they sometimes took refuge in an impenetrable obscurity. It will suffice to refer to Calvin's celebrated pronouncement upon the problem of interest. Long under consideration and proclaimed after much hesitation, it gave room for two diametrically opposite deductions: on the one hand that the exaction of interest was not forbidden under all circumstances but that it must not be pressed so far as to

[17] *Protestant Ethic,* p. 159.

amount to 'usury'; on the other, that any interest rates at all were permissible.

Moreover, we know nothing of the impact of these varying *dicta* on their readers; even if Baxter was more imbued with the 'spirit of capitalism' than St. Paul or Thomas Aquinas, the effect of this difference upon the conduct of men may well have been nil.

Irrespective of whether the difference of degree which Weber postulates between Baxter and the earlier church fathers corresponds to the facts, Baxter's attitude to economic activity is just as divided as, for instance, Wesley's or Fox's. Riches—and even Weber has to admit this—are denounced just as vigorously as diligence and the ascetic life are extolled. As with the other great Puritan writers, to be rich is always a danger if not actually an offence in itself. Wealth already attained is just as pernicious as the striving to amass wealth. Men are tempted to stray into paths other than those prescribed by God, they become worldly, and the love of the Kingdom of God vanishes.

Furthermore, Baxter's conception of the 'calling' has no connection with the notion that success in worldly affairs and the increase of business and fortune are a mark of God's favour or a foretaste of the joys that await the faithful in Heaven. Man shall not, he declares, choose the vocation in life that promises the maximum advantage in money or esteem, but that in which he can best serve God and most easily avoid sin. And there is yet another obligation. Man must devote himself to those activities which best conduce to the public weal, which produce the greatest social benefit. It does not help that he employs exclusively lawful means and becomes rich through the pursuit of his calling. The love of riches is unlawful, whatever the means. It is no incitement to unrestricted economic individualism that Baxter intends, but an exhortation to labour, under strict moral laws, for the general good. Every man shall be content with his lot and shall resolutely persist in useful endeavour, be the reward what it may. The toleration of one's

37

lot cannot be plausibly represented as a lifegiving element in the 'spirit of capitalism'. The fervour with which the special virtues of poverty are depicted makes it seem more appropriate to apply the Marxist cliché that religion was the opium of the people.

More interesting than the passages in which Baxter can best be described as purely anti-capitalistic are those where he takes a more benevolent view of the operations of businessmen and entrepreneurs. For it is here that there emerges most clearly the dilemma between religion and economic activity, in which Baxter and the other Puritan fathers found themselves. What we find is not a religious teacher urging disciples to address themselves to trade and other forms of enterprise and to win God's favour by success in such activities; on the contrary, it is a leader of the congregation finding that the disciples already converted or receptive to his evangelical message consist very largely of businessmen and industrialists. Sensing the claims of practical life, he seeks to resolve the predicament by clarifying the moral conditions under which a prosperous, even wealthy, businessman may, despite success and wealth, become a good Christian. It is customary to say that a man who has become rich by business has made good use of his time, declares Baxter. But since it is the Kingdom of Heaven, closeness to God, a holy life, and a death tempered by rejoicing and confidence that we aim to achieve, should we not eagerly devote our time to these ends instead? The businessman must obey the law; must seek first and foremost to act for the common good; must follow the prices dictated by public opinion and the market and not raise his price because a commodity is greatly coveted by someone; must not initiate or conduct any monopolistic enterprise which tends to enrich him at the expense of the community.

Those businessmen who, in order to gain salvation, sought to follow the edicts of Baxter—or Fox or Wesley or Penn— might continue their activities. To God nothing was impossible. Even the rich man *might* win grace. But if religion had any relevance at all, the conduct of business must have been accompanied by anxiety, perpetual disquietude of conscience, and great frustration engendered by moral injunctions. It may well be that, as with the requiem masses sought by Catholics, the religious conceptions of the Puritans sometimes provide an explanation of their large donations of money. To the Puritans, riches were so perilous that absolution must be obtained by giving away money, and above all by making donations for ecclesiastical purposes. But that being so, it indicates an attitude quite the reverse of what on any reasonable interpretation could be termed capitalistic.

One of the most widely read religious writers was Bunyan; enormous editions of his *Pilgrim's Progress* and *Life and Death of Mr. Badman* were printed. How does he deal with economic activity and the day-to-day observance of duty in general? Christian forsakes his family and his trade to seek the Kingdom of Heaven. In the course of his pilgrimage he meets a succession of persons representing the most common vices. They seek to entice him back into ordinary life. But he withstands the test. Years later, his wife and children follow his example. One of the vices that must be forsworn is avarice, the lust for riches. Christian walks proudly past the alluring silver-mine, and those of his companions who succumb to the temptations of illusory wealth are buried in the mine and forfeit their celestial bliss. The businessmen whom Christian and his companion Faithful meet in Vanity Fair are wicked men, striving to become rich by satisfying men's desire for beautiful but vain objects. To renounce the world, not to serve it by fulfilling the daily call, is the way to salvation.

The idea of bringing God into worldly affairs, of regarding success and riches as a sign of piety and godliness is most emphatically rejected by Bunyan. The allegorical figure which represents the love of gold asks why a priest or a merchant should not, through displaying godliness, secure advancement and a larger income. The former thereby becomes a more able preacher and thus pursues his calling. The latter may perhaps get a rich wife and better customers by displaying this virtue; and godliness *is* a virtue irrespective of why it is practised. Bunyan makes Christian repudiate such ideas. If it is unseemly to follow Christ for the sake of one's daily bread, then how infamous it is to make of religion and Christ the Lord a cloak under which to seek riches and worldly esteem. He who puts on piety and godliness for the sake of the world may just as well cast them off in favour of worldly success. This is the piety of Judas Iscariot, a piety tainted by lucre. The true piety is not of this world, and only by renunciation of this world can it be achieved. 'Love not the world, neither the things that are in the world. If any man love the world, the love of the Father is not in him. For all that is in the world, the lust of the flesh, and the lust of the eyes, and the pride of life, is not of the Father, but is of the world. And the world passeth away, and the lust thereof: but he that doeth the will of God abideth for ever.'

These words from the First Epistle of John (2, xv–xvii) are *not* cited by Bunyan, but if there is any passage of the Bible that could be taken as a maxim for the pilgrimages of Christian and his wife, it would be difficult to find one that better epitomised the basic idea of both books. Estrangement from this world, and the avoidance of sin by means of wholly spiritual exertions, two of the strongest themes of Puritanism—and perhaps especially of Pietism—come very much into their own in Bunyan. There is nothing of that 'worldly asceticism' which, according to Weber, so sharply differentiated the Puritan movements from Catholicism.

In Mr. Badman it is usury, unjust prices, covetousness and avarice, all of them 'most commonly committed by men of trade' that are chiefly castigated. Mr. Badman is the shopkeeper who 'bites and pinches the poor'. Trade and traders represent evil.

In general, then, if there emerges from the most important writers and preachers of the various Puritan sects a single common factor in their approach to business life and economic

activity, it is the exhortation to subordinate them to the require-
ments of Christian morality; and to moderate what are regarded as excesses, in the form not only of unjust prices and
morally reprehensible transactions but also of rising turnover
and expanding business. It is the picture of the small trader
or craftsman, conducting his enterprise after the fashion of a
good Christian, thinking of the general good, being kind to the
poor, honourable in all transactions, free of the aspiration to
enlarge his business and gain riches, that is portrayed as the
ideal. The inculcation of habits of diligence and thrift was
sought, but so too of contentment and restraint. It was made
quite clear that special exertions were demanded of the wealthy
and successful if they were to win salvation.

Tawney's observations about Baxter are much the same as
those put forward here. Nevertheless he reaches the conclusion
that 'the capitalist spirit,' though 'as old as history, found in
certain aspects of Puritanism a tonic which braced its energies
and fortified its already vigorous temper.' [18] How is this possible? It is made possible by means of a somersault in the best
Weberian style. The Puritans tried to foster Christian morals
and virtuous habits in their followers amongst the trading
and industrial communities; they strove to evolve 'a Christian
casuistry of economic conduct'. Unquestionably, this ought to
have impeded rather than promoted a capitalistic trend. But,
says Tawney, it did not succeed; and the roots of this failure
are to be found not merely in the obstacles created by an
economic environment that became ever more hostile as that
capitalistic trend progressed, but primarily in 'the soul of Puritanism itself'. The Puritans did not range themselves against
the admonitions of the traditional Christian ethic concerning
the 'numberless disguises assumed by the sin which sticketh
fast between buying and selling,' writes Tawney. Instead, the
Puritan character offered 'a polished surface on which these
ghostly admonitions could find no enduring foot-hold. The
rules of Christian morality elaborated by Baxter were subtle

[18] *Religion and the Rise of Capitalism,* pp. 226—7.

and sincere. But they were like seeds carried by birds from a distant and fertile plain and dropped upon a glacier. They were at once embalmed and sterilized in a river of ice.' [19] In Tawney's view, this icy soil was the true and genuine Puritan spirit which the Puritan fathers sought in vain to cultivate. Puritanism in some other and more capitalistic sense, by virtue of its superior strength over the doctrines proclaimed by its founders and greatest preachers, becomes the capitalistic spirit's principal source of power, even if not its creator as Weber alleged.

Could anything offer a better demonstration than this concoction, coming as it does from so brilliant a writer as Tawney, of how the whole concept of the contribution of Puritan teachings to the rise of Capitalism has led to a hopeless morass of loose thinking, generalisations and re-interpretations. If we accept Tawney's view that no success was achieved by the efforts to induce entrepreneurs and merchants to make it their first duty to satisfy the demands of Christian morality and the common good, indeed deliberately to limit the scope of their operations and to shun riches (and there is good reason to agree with Tawney on this point), then the obvious conclusion is quite different from his: the economic views of the Puritans neither encouraged nor obstructed the spirit of capitalism. This spirit existed and throve quite independently of religious belief. Insofar as successful businessmen were also members of Puritan sects, they were not impelled to economic transactions by their religion. But sometimes they tried to construe these transactions, both to themselves and to others, in as favourable a religious light as possible; they thereby provided, to the confusion of posterity, an impression of a link that did not exist.

What was this true and genuine Puritanism, evidently so different from that preached by the foremost Puritan teachers? On what religious concepts was it based?

Neither Weber nor Tawney leaves us entirely without guidance

[19] *Ibid.*, p. 226.

on these important questions. The starting-point is the special Calvinist idea of vocation, the concept of the 'calling'. This idea, say Weber and Tawney, rested on Calvin's doctrine of election and predestination.[20] Energy in daily work and success in his trade or vocation were signs that the individual was of the company chosen for salvation. And so in the long run, no matter how the Puritan fathers preached of the perils and the curse of riches, it was religion that inspired adherents of the Reformed church to unremitting diligence and the relentless accumulation of riches.

Is this view correct?

We can begin by noticing that Weber has difficulty in making up his mind on an extremely important point. Was success in his chosen work only a *sign* that the diligent person was of the elect, or was the practice of this virtue also a *means* of winning salvation? The former hypothesis is entirely consistent with the doctrine of predestination, although far from indispensable to it. The latter is logically incompatible with the doctrine of predetermined election: in His infinite knowledge and wisdom, God must have foreseen the attempt to influence His decision. Weber vacillates between the two ideas. The Calvinist, he says, 'himself creates his own salvation,' but adds for safety's sake 'or, as would be more correct, the conviction of it'. A fundamental distinction is thus neatly reduced to a mere matter of relative precision in phraseology. 'However useless good works might be as a means of attaining salvation... they are in-

---

[20] On predestination and the 'calling,' see *Religion and Rise of Capitalism*, pp. 108, 240 ff.; *Protestant Ethic*, pp. 79 ff., 98 ff., 109 ff. and *Gesammelte Aufsätze*, pp. 43, 89, 103 ff., 108 ff., 111; Gunsteren, *op. cit.*, p. 160 ff.; Clemmensen, *op. cit.*, p. 60 ff.; Kraus, *op. cit.*, pp. 230, 234. For a criticism of Tawney, see in particular, Kraus, p. 117. See also B. A. Fuchs, *Der Geist der bürgerlich-kapitalistischen Gesellschaft* (1914), esp. p. 39 f. n. 29; Sombart, *Der Bourgeois;* A. Hyma, 'Calvinism and Capitalism, 1555—1700,' *Journal of Modern History*, Vol. X (1938), pp. 321—43. An unpublished essay, from 1943, by Börje Hansson, 'Kritisk granskning av Max Webers Die Protestantische Ethik,' which the author most kindly put at my disposal, has also been particularly drawn upon in this section.

dispensable as a sign of election. They are the technical means, not of purchasing salvation, but of getting rid of the fear of damnation.' There follows a characteristic *non sequitur:* 'in practice this means that God helps those who help themselves.'[21]

Weber admits that the idea of predestination did not always give birth to diligence and 'worldly asceticism'. Another and quite contrary contingency is open, and this second solution comes close to Lutheranism. Here, religious experience is expressed by a *Gefühlskultur,* coloured by mysticism, rather than in the trade and worldly activity of Calvinism. He makes no attempt, however, to explain why this latter outcome should be found simply amongst the Calvinists, referring to it instead as a matter of common knowledge, undisputed and indisputable.

His whole exposition of the concept of predestination and the ethos of vocation, of the 'sanctity of labour' in Calvinism, is, to put it mildly, of dubious validity. The concept of predestination was already fully evolved in St. Paul, and it was urged with much vigour by Augustine, in whose theology the doctrine of election, of the few chosen for salvation, was a central principle. Why it should be only in Calvin and Calvinism, not in St. Paul, Augustine or Luther, that the idea of the 'sanctity of labour' came to be used, Weber is unable to explain. In fact, Calvin reveals not the faintest trace of any conception of the 'sanctity of labour,' of the prospect of changing God's decision, once made, or of obtaining knowledge of that decision through the medium of worldly success. For Calvin predestination was an inevitable consequence of the omniscience and infinite wisdom of God. To seek to influence or discover God's decision by means of work and worldly deeds was improper. Inner spiritual intuition was for Calvin as much as for Paul the only means of learning God's decision. To influence the decision in any way was unthinkable: God, who had foreseen and foreordained all, would also have foreseen this attempt to influence Him. Furthermore, predestination, both in Augustine and Calvin,

[21] *Protestant Ethic,* p. 115.

had nothing to do with the goodness or wickedness of the individual or with good or wicked deeds. All men are wicked, born in original sin; all are doomed to perdition. But in His inscrutable mercy and to the glory of His holy name, God has chosen certain people for salvation.

Weber suggests that the concept of the 'calling,' the idea that God's decision can be influenced, appears in later Calvinist theologians. As late as 1647, at all events, the Confession of Westminster—which Weber himself quotes—clings to the same conception of predestination as Calvin held: 'Those of mankind that are predestinated unto life, God before the foundation of the world was laid, according to His eternal and immutable purpose, and the secret counsel and good pleasure of His will, hath chosen in Christ unto everlasting glory, out of His mere free grace and love, without any foresight of faith or good works, or perseverance in either of them, or any other thing in the creature as conditions, or causes moving Him thereunto, and all to the praise of His glorious grace.' [22] The others, those doomed to perdition, have been chosen in the same manner, without reference to deeds or faith, 'for the glory of His sovereign power over His creatures'. The same idea, expressed with varying degrees of clarity, can be found amongst the great Free church preachers, in Wesley, Fox, Baxter, and Bunyan.

Unable to find in Calvin any support for his theory of the importance for the 'sanctity of labour' of the concept of predestination, Weber turns instead to the ordinary Calvinist believer. Here is the same arbitrary method as can be seen in later writers: in van Gunsteren, when he deals with the same topic; in Tawney, both in his treatment of the doctrine of predestination and on the question of that true, genuine Puritan spirit, so utterly opposed to what the Puritan fathers sought to inculcate. The world was to be sanctified by toil and struggle. And the proof that Calvin's doctrine of predestination, so alien to this conception, could lead to this conclusion? Why, Cal-

[22] Quoted *Protestant Ethic*, p. 100.

vinism, with all its renunciation of personal gain, is so tremendously practical. The proposition that was to be proved must itself serve as proof.

Let us for a moment ignore the question of whether the ordinary Calvinist believer, despite Calvin and the later Calvinist preachers, regarded his industriousness as the sign that he was chosen, and indeed as a means of becoming chosen. Let us suppose that Weber, Tawney and van Gunsteren are right on this point. Their proof still does not hold. If, contrary to the essential tenets of Calvinist doctrine, the adherents of that doctrine adopt the belief suggested and then turn it into a vital component of their religious faith, does this not indicate a relationship directly the reverse of that suggested by Weber, Tawney and van Gunsteren? Does it not indicate that hardworking, economically successful men have elevated their industry and prosperity into religious virtue; that the ordinary civic virtues such as diligence, thrift and honesty in business have come to form an element of the faith of the believer? If, of course, a connection needs to be assumed at all.

In the earlier references to Brentano and Robertson[23] it was shown how Weber wrongly assumes that the double connotation in the word 'calling' (*Beruf*) is the sole property of Calvinism; the same double meaning is to be found, long before the Reformation, in the corresponding words of several languages. Something similar occurs in his account of predestination and industry, where the expression *gute Werke* is used. Tawney speaks of 'good works' in the same way. These two expressions may signify both good deeds in the ordinary religious and ethical sense of 'doing good,' or they may alternatively denote a 'good job of work'. In the one connotation, only the industrious and persevering can boast of good works, *gute Werke*. In the other—surely far more customary and appropriate in religion—even the laziest and most incompetent can pride himself on his good deeds.

It is obviously this latter meaning that Calvin, Wesley, Fox,

[23] See above, pp. 13, 17.

46

Penn and Baxter generally intend when they use the expression. In this they are following St. Paul. It is precisely this meaning that is apparent in the First Epistle to Timothy (6, xvii–xviii) and which guided the Free Church fathers in the 16th, 17th and 18th centuries. After denouncing the pursuit of riches—'for we brought nothing into this world, and it is certain we can carry nothing out'—and asserting the importance of contentment, St. Paul exhorts those who are already rich 'that they do good, that they be rich in good works'; by this means they shall avoid entrusting their hopes to the vain riches of this world and escape the dangers that riches involve.

At times St. Paul and the Calvinist writers are guilty, as we saw Baxter to be, of slipping into the connotation of 'a good job of work' as suggested by Weber. But there is no hint of 'unrelenting zeal' or of struggle to acquire riches as a sign of election or Divine love. The counsel of Baxter, Wesley, Fox and Penn—as well as St. Paul—in this kind of context includes no admonition to seek advancement and 'fight one's way forward,' but to remain in the station to which one has been called, industrious, faithful and content with one's lot. Perform your daily tasks without striving for advancement and riches, and devote your free time to serving God and doing good—this was the precept that circumscribed the business activities of so many Quakers. The mystically tinged *Gefühlskultur* which Weber alleged to be the property of Catholicism and Lutheran evangelism was by no means absent among the Puritans.

But we certainly do not find it in Benjamin Franklin, or in the great American captains of industry a hundred years later. The 'capitalistic spirit' which they exhibit is not a culmination of the Puritanism encountered in the great fathers of the free sects. On the contrary, the feature that stands out is the utter dissimilarity of the one from the other.

Before dealing with this topic, however, a few words need to be said about the general trends of economic thought embraced in the overall evolution of ideas both before and after the Reformation. Naturally, they can only be discussed briefly. To omit them from the argument entirely, however, would be unduly to isolate our problems from their general context.

2. SECULARISATION AND THE IDEOLOGICAL REVOLUTION

The opinion held by Sombart, Brentano, Robertson, Tawney and Kraus, to the effect that 'capitalism' and the 'capitalistic spirit' existed long before the Reformation, is essentially correct. It is also true that, by degrees, substantial changes had taken place in the Catholic outlook even before the Reformation. There was scarcely a single field in which the ideas of the Catholic church had remained stationary. Some manifestations of their evolution may be indicated by a simple catalogue of developments: the Platonic-Aristotelian controversy among the schoolmen—Anselm towards the end of the 11th century, Abelard, Bernard of Clairvaux and Peter Lombard around the mid-12th century, Bonaventura a hundred years later; the Franciscan and Benedictine exhortations to thrift and joy in labour; the zeal of the Jesuits in business as in other affairs; Wyclif and his Lollards, preaching that all property is God's, and that the right to use it is conjoined with the obligation to maintain it faithfully and improve it. The pre-Reformation Catholic world of ideas holds the product of centuries of debate, internal struggles, new ideas and successive emancipation from old bonds. Neither in its Protestant nor its Reformed guise did the Reformation involve any sudden ideological break with the past. Its roots reach far back into pre-Reformation currents of thought, accepted or resisted within the mother church. Its world of ideas is not new. Viewed in the perspective of the history of ideas as a whole, the element of divergence from the corresponding Catholic world was from the beginning exceedingly slight.[24]

[24] For the development of ideas in the Catholic church, see Latourette, *op. cit.*, pp. 495 ff., 622 ff., 684 ff.; P. Hazard, *La crise de la conscience*

However, the fact that it is possible both to observe changes taking place in this world of ecclesiastical ideas long before the Reformation (including, as Sombart, Tawney and Robertson noted, some broadening of outlook in the field of economic thought) and to discuss the occurrence of 'capitalism' and the 'capitalistic spirit' in, for example, the 14th and 15th centuries does not by any means signify a necessary connection between the two phenomena. In fact, a 'spirit of capitalism' manifested itself in the Italian merchant cities and the Hanseatic League, in the textile industry (though this was scarcely 'capitalistic' in the sense of occasioning extensive mobilisation of capital), and the mining industry long before changes of opinion about usury and other economic phenomena can even have started seriously to affect the Catholic outlook, let alone become a motivating force in practical economic conduct. The decisive circumstances must have lain in something other than the reorientation of religious concepts.

Insofar as this period did witness changes in the climate of opinion of such a nature as to influence economic developments, they took place not, as Weber supposes, solely *inside* the framework of religious beliefs, but *outside* it as well. Through the Renaissance and the great geographical discoveries, the contacts with the Arab kingdoms and later with other cultures, the creation of new centres of learning, the disintegration of the feudal system or its absorption into the great principalities, the new theories of the state—in a variety of ways and through a variety of media, opinions were moulded and changed. All the indications are that it was a fairly lengthy and gradual process touching almost all branches of the culture of western and northern Europe. All attempts to assign it to a definite period, e.g., pre- or post-Reformation, are doomed to failure. To the extent that a 'new spirit' begins to reveal itself in earnest

européenne, 1680—1715 (1935) and *La pensée européenne au XVIIIᵉ siècle*, I—II (1946); and R. H. Banton, 'Changing Ideas and Ideals in the Sixteenth Century,' *Journal of Modern History*, Vol. VIII (1936), pp. 419—43.

in the 15th and 16th centuries, it embraced well-nigh every aspect of the life of the community. This new spirit of creativeness, of protest against the old order, of inquiry and widening horizons, was a feature shared in common by economic progress, political and cultural trends, and the break with Catholicism. The great explorers of Spain and Portugal, though Catholics, were animated by it just as much as the Reformed or Lutheran seafarers of England and the Netherlands, and the mercantile houses of Lisbon just as much as those of Amsterdam and London.

The movement is a general one, whether manifested in exhortations to thrift and diligence or in demands for economic individualism, political freedom and the 'social' view of life.[25] The situation in the 17th and 18th centuries is similar. Different systems of thought flow into and contend with each other, recombining in new syntheses that are absorbed into the broad currents of the main stream of ideas. A number of the views on various topics held in common by Fox, Penn, Wesley and other leaders of the sects are also met with in strictly 'worldly' writers, first the mercantilists, then the philosophers of the Age of Enlightenment, the physiocrats and the early liberals. Quesnay, Turgot, Locke, Hume, Adam Smith, Montesquieu—even a work with so Weberesque an approach as Warner's—apparently thought it impossible to put the religious teachers in their proper context without referring to the general ideological currents which these names represent. Grubb, for example, finds it instructive to study the points of similarity and contrast between Adam Smith and Quaker publicists. Although the approach to particular problems is in certain respects very dissi-

[25] On this general movement of ideas discussed in the pages that follow, see, *inter alia*, E. F. Heckscher, *Mercantilism*, G. Bryson, *Man and Society. The Scottish Inquiry of the Eighteenth Century* (1945), pp. 5 ff., 25 ff., H. McLachlan, *English Education under the Test Acts* (1931), esp. p. 27, Ashton, *op. cit.*, p. 15 ff., H. Wish, *Society and Thought in Modern America*, I—II (1952), J. T. Adams, *The Epic of America* (1954). See also the works cited on p. 69 *n.* 54 below.

milar, common features deriving from the general spirit of the age can be perceived.[26]

Gladys Bryson, who studied the contribution of Scotland to social and economic thought in the 18th century, emphasised the great importance of the philosophy of the Enlightenment and of more liberal conceptions to the vigour that Scottish cultural development began to display at that time. How much this had to do with contemporary social and economic progress it is impossible to determine. Particularly interesting, however, is the discovery that this progress makes its appearance *after* the dominating influence of Calvinism had been overthrown, *after* other systems of thought, often wholly secular, had replaced the religious conceptions or transformed them beyond recognition, and *after* dogma, austerity and the puritanical element had vanished or become so enfeebled as to be negligible. The galaxy of great teachers at Glasgow University and elsewhere, lecturing in moral philosophy as well as economic theory, mathematics and everyday business practice (Ferguson, Moore, Leechmann, Hutcheson, Hume, Smith, and Dugald Stewart) demanded freedom from all external authority, especially that of religion, in the selection of moral and practical criteria.[27]

This emancipation from moral precepts dictated by religion was perhaps the most striking general characteristic of Scottish education, not only at the universities but also at lesser seats of learning. Of its role in a wider context it is obviously difficult to form any very definite impression. That Scotland represented a new spirit, a 'new deal,' so to speak, in scholarship and education, and that this exercised a substantial influence on the whole of English education in the second half of the 18th century, however, can be asserted with confidence. It was the spirit that we customarily associate with the word 'Enlightenment': free thought, free inquiry, free experiment. Joseph Black, professor of chemistry first at Glasgow and then at Edinburgh University,

26 I. Grubb, *op. cit., passim.*
27 Bryson, *op. cit.*

51

surely deserves more credit for his share in the experimental work that produced the great inventions than a whole multitude of Free church fathers with their cries for diligence and thrift.[28]

The universities of New England were similarly emancipating themselves during this period. Harvard and the newly established Yale began to plead the case for the philosophy of the Enlightenment and the empiricism of the natural sciences, and to claim independence from religious authority. The orthodox came to regard them as advocates of a dangerous worldliness, representatives of wickedness clad in the suits of learning.

At the beginning of the 18th century, Harvard, which was regarded as the chief bulwark of Puritanism, was 'taken over' by Anglican circles—and its greatness dates from this time. By the end of the 17th century, increased immigration had already loosened the grip of the sects on the people. The orthodox religious dogmas were being forced to yield. Enlightenment concepts of reason and natural order flooded in. When George Whitefield, the famous Methodist leader, visited New England, he found himself loved by the masses but coldly received by the university, this 'godless Harvard,' as he called it. In the lists of recommended reading, the name of Locke appeared as one of the most important writers. The students were advised to learn French so that they might meet the ideas of the Enlightenment directly at their source.

By the middle of the 18th century, Yale too was to be revealed as similarly 'godless' from the Calvinist point of view. At King's College—later to become Columbia University, New York—Samuel Johnson reigned, an open enemy of what he regarded as Calvinistic fanaticism. Under the pressure both of other religious movements and of 'worldly' influences, the Congregationalist church in New England lost its old position; church and state were separated in Connecticut in 1818 and

[28] Black's pupils included not only the celebrated Watt, but also James Keir, chemist of the glass industry and that many-sided inventor and innovator, Archibald Cochran, Earl of Dundonald. See Bryson, *op. cit.*

in 1833 Massachusetts followed suit. This, writes James Truslow Adams, was the outward and visible sign of a change that had long been under way: 'the old Puritan theology and fervor had been dying for many a day.'[29] In every department of life, the break with the old Puritan spirit was asserting itself: in the sciences (Franklin's explanation of the phenomenon of lightning and his invention of the lightning conductor were no mean contributions to the extinction of traditional religious conceptions), in art and music and literature, in personal social intercourse, in habits and customs.

This break with the past—with the 'true' Puritan spirit— was not solely the work of the Enlightenment or of secularised philosophies of life generally. New religious faiths played their part as well. As Wright points out, not even the first Puritan immigrants had all been Calvinists.[30] In New England the influence of various forms of Arminianism was substantial, and in the second half of the 18th century was growing.[31] The Arminians taught that men were born with the capacity for both sinful and righteous lives; they rejected Calvin's doctrine that all men were bound by original sin and that God had chosen a few for salvation and condemned the rest to eternal perdition; they preached free will and rejected predestination. The Anglican church was strongly influenced by Arminianism, as also was the Methodist movement, without the fact being directly acknowledged. Admittedly, men like Samuel Johnson strenuously denied that they were Arminians; but it was evident that though they refused the name they accepted the doctrine.[32] Channing's Unitarianism, with its more cheerful view of life, its blending of both the 'rationalist' and the 'romantic' elements in the Enlightenment, its combination of piety and tolerance,

---

[29] J. T. Adams, op. cit., p. 158.

[30] C. Wright, The Beginnings of Unitarianism in America (1955), pp. 11 f., 15.

[31] Arminianism originated with Jacob Arminius, founder of a Dutch sect, at the end of the 16th century.

[32] Wright, op. cit., p. 58.

was a culmination of these movements.[33] With Channing, Christianity became the religion of reason and God the principle of reason. Many men of the Enlightenment discarded God and Christianity in the name of reason. But Channing declared that for him God simply *was* reason: 'Christianity is a rational religion. Were it not so, I should be ashamed to profess it.' We must 'never forget that our rational nature is the greatest gift of God'. If, he continues 'I could not be a Christian without ceasing to be rational, I should not hesitate as to my choice...'[34] Thus could the man of the Enlightenment remain reconciled with God; he very neatly turned God into the foremost of the Men of the Enlightenment.

Few others attacked Calvin, Calvinism, and thus the whole Puritan tradition, as violently as did Channing. Few assailed so forcefully the moral doctrine of Calvinism, the concept of original sin and predestination. Few equalled Channing's vigour —but he was certainly not alone. At the beginning of the 19th century the old Puritan theology and Puritan zeal, to repeat the quotation from James Truslow Adams, had 'been dying for many a day'.

The existence of a multiplicity of different sects in the United States enforced in many important fields a measure of cooperation 'above' religion, as it were. In order to unite for the achievement of common ends, religious conflicts had to be put aside—and this frequently aided the process of secularisation and the loosening of doctrinaire Puritan bonds. Benjamin Franklin himself supplies one example. In a circular letter of 1743, he sketched the broad outlines of an American philosophical society which, in its headquarters at Philadelphia, was to consist of a physicist, a botanist, a mathematician, a chemist, a geographer, one representative of natural philosophy in general, and one of mechanics. The aims of the society were set

[33] *The Works of William Ellery Channing, D. D.* (New Ed. 1840). See in particular p. 74 ff. (Against Calvinism), p. 137 ff. (On Property), p. 307 ff. (Unitarian Christianity), p. 432 ff. (Christianity a Rational Religion).

[34] *Ibid.,* p. 433—4.

54

entirely on the plane of natural science, medicine and philosophy. The trustees of the 'academy' which was founded some years later and became the University of Pennsylvania in 1791, included a representative of every sect in the state. The consequence was pacification, if not utter passivity, in the sphere of religious education; languages and natural science became the chief interests. William and Mary College, the oldest university in the United States after Harvard, was far removed from genuine Puritanism when Thomas Jefferson was a student there in the early 1760s. Dances, the theatre, horse racing, carousals and love affairs, if not exactly the order of the day, were at all events not unusual.

This brings us to the secularised era, entirely divorced from Puritanism, of Thomas Jefferson and Benjamin Franklin.

3. BENJAMIN FRANKLIN

The 'spirit of capitalism' emanating from Protestantism generally and the Puritan sects in particular reached its culmination, says Weber, in Benjamin Franklin. Weber has to admit, however, that this culmination was 'secularised,' and that Franklin's thought and outlook on life were in large measure the fruit of the Enlightenment. This admission is in itself so damaging that Weber's thesis really falls to the ground. If the doctrines of Protestantism generally and the Puritan sects in particular are regarded as the source of the 'spirit of capitalism,' if purely religious conceptions are claimed to be the decisive factor, then it is clearly preposterous to declare that this spirit reaches full maturity and manifests itself most vigorously in someone who in certain vital respects is far removed from these conceptions and in whose outlook entirely different patterns of thought predominate. If Protestantism only became 'truly capitalistic' when supplemented, at the expense of some of its own ideas, by concepts of quite different origin, then in the centuries before Franklin it cannot of itself possibly have possessed to any appreciable extent the power ascribed to it by Weber, i.e. that it imparted a forward impetus to economic trends and thus constituted a source of the 'spirit of capitalism'.

And in reality the dominant themes in Franklin's utterances are those of the Enlightenment, of secularisation. That he was religious in the sense that he believed in God is beyond all doubt. But although Franklin was brought up in the Calvinist creed, his particular religious strain did not bear the impress of Calvinism, nor was it perceptibly Puritan. On the contrary, the outstanding characteristic of Franklin was his thorough emancipation. He allowed himself to be elected to the Pennsylvania assembly as a representative of the Quakers, although openly admitting that he did not share the Quakers' religious views. He published Whitefield's writings, gave him financial support and admired the vigour of the message he preached, although express'y declaring that he did not share his beliefs for a moment. One episode is illuminating. When Whitefield on one occasion thanks Franklin for his invitation to use his house and says that this friendly act shall not go unrewarded if the sacrifice was made for Christ's sake, Franklin replies that Whitefield should not deceive himself. 'It was not for Christ's sake, but for your sake.' [35] In his autobiography Franklin adds that, well aware of the proclivity of holy men to shift the burden of gratitude from their own shoulders and place it in heaven, he considered that by this rejoinder he had 'contrived to fix it on earth'.[36]

Franklin's approach to religious problems is described in his autobiography. Early in life he had ceased to participate in public religious meetings. The Sabbath was his time for study and research. Certain of the tenets of Presbyterian doctrine seemed to him clearly 'unintelligible, others doubtful'. But he never doubted the existence of God, or that God created the world and governed it by His Providence, that the form of piety most pleasing to God was to do good, and that sin would be punished and virtue rewarded. This was the core of all

[35] *Autobiography,* p. 137. [36] *Ibid.,* p. 137.

56

religious faiths; therefore they could all be respected though the regree of respect might vary according to their success in inculcating high moral standards. The vital criterion of the worth of a religious doctrine is morality, not the form or intensity of belief. Franklin made it a guiding principle to avoid all discussions that might offend religious susceptibilities. 'In my states everyone may be devout after his fashion,' was a rule that he heartily espoused.

Franklin relates how at the beginning of the 1730s he had had notions of founding a new 'religion'. He believed his studies to have disclosed that the affairs of the world were directed by parties; that these parties served only their own immediate interests; that their conflicting interests caused confusion; that the determination of each individual to pursue his personal interest in the last resort caused new parties to be formed and thus made confusion worse confounded; and that only a few figures in public life actively tried to serve the interests of the nation as a whole. In order to cure this evil he wanted to create a 'United Party for Virtue, by forming the virtues and good men of all nations into a regular body'.[37] The drafts which Franklin had made at the time when he wrote his autobiography have now all been lost, with one exception. The one that survives shows that his basic idea was to devise a creed 'containing, as I thought, the essentials of every known religion and being free of everything that might shock the professors of any religion'.[38] Note the faint sneer in the phraseology. The ingredients of this religion were the simplest possible, acceptable alike to Puritans, Lutherans, Catholics, and presumably Mohammedans too. 'That there is one God who made all things. That he governs the world by his providence. That he ought to be worshiped by adoration, prayer and thanksgiving. But that the most acceptable service of God is doing good to man. That the soul is immortal. And that God will certainly reward virtue and punish vice, either here or hereafter.'[39]

[37] *Ibid.*, p. 119. [38] *Ibid.*, p. 119. [39] *Ibid.*, p. 119.

Virtue, in this context, was virtue of the utmost generality, the mere absence of sin and selfishness.

But it is not simply this oecumenical strain, this tolerance, making a strict piety in the Puritan sense impossible, that is of importance in this context. Neither in his personal habits of life nor in his advice to other people did Franklin exhibit anything of the concept of the 'calling'. He regarded diligence and thrift as useful. But Franklin was no champion of unremitting labour in response to a 'call'. For his own part, he confesses that at an early age he had planned to make, as quickly as possible, a fortune large enough to enable him to retire and occupy himself with public duties and intellectual and scientific interests. Excess in food and drink he considered reprehensible. But his reason was not that men thereby surrendered their souls to the world and centred their thoughts on things temporal, 'the flesh'. It is not the religious preacher vigilant to uphold piety who is speaking, but the scientist interested in medical problems. 'Rules of Health and Long Life' is what he calls his advice on this subject in *Poor Richard;*[40] it might have been copied word for word from a modern doctor's admonitions on the hazards of obesity. The individual should eat and drink exactly as much as suits his constitution, having regard to the well-being of the body and vigour of the spirit. The sedentary worker should eat less than the manual worker, for the digestion of the former is not as good. Different ages and different conditions of health require different quantities. Similarly with people of varying general disposition: what is too much for a phlegmatic is insufficient for a choleric. One should eat because it is necessary for the health, not gorge to gratify the senses, for greed does not know where necessity ends.

Franklin himself was no consistent despiser of the table. On various occasions he remarks that he has eaten an excellent dinner and drunk a good glass of wine. A trifle shocked when his wife one day produced a bowl of Chinese porcelain and

[40] *Writings of Benjamin Franklin,* Vol. II, p. 227 (ed. by A. H. Smyth, 1905).

a silver spoon for his table, he soon made himself at ease with this 'luxury'. 'This was the first appearance of plate and china in our house, which afterwards, in a course of years, as our wealth increas'd, augmented gradually to several hundred pounds in value.' [41]

The general rules of life that Franklin set up for himself, the virtues that he wished to practise, are not in the least peculiarly Puritan. There is not one which would not have fitted admirably into some edifying primer for school children in any country at all—Calvinist, Lutheran or Catholic. There is *temperance:* 'eat not to dullness; drink not to elevation. There are also *silence:* speak not but what may benefit others or yourself; avoid trifling conversation; *order:* let all your things have their place; let each part of your business have its time; *resolution:* resolve to perform what you ought; perform without fail what you resolve; *frugality:* make no expense but to do good to others or yourself; *industry:* lose no time; be always employ'd in something useful; cut off all unnecessary actions; *sincerity; justice; moderation; cleanliness; tranquillity; humility* and *chastity:* rarely use venery but for health or offspring, never to dullness, weakness, or the injury of your own or another's peace or reputation'.[42] Franklin's enlightened attitude and 'rationalism' in sexual matters generally is noteworthy and quite free from any of the overtones usually associated with 'Puritanism' in this context.

Franklin passes the following verdict on these precepts: 'It will be remark'd that, tho' my scheme was not wholly without religion, there was in it no mark of any of the distinguishing tenets of any particular sect.' [43] He deliberately tried to avoid this. The virtues he wished to infuse in others and to practise himself were such as would fit all religions.

In his *Advice to a Young Tradesman* Franklin lays down the qualities which he considers essential for success in business.

[41] *Autobiography,* p. 104.
[42] *Ibid.,* pp. 107—8.
[43] *Ibid,* p. 115.

There is not a word to suggest that economic activity is a duty before God or success a mark of His favour. The only mention of a higher power is when Franklin declares that he who follows his advice will become rich, assuming that Providence has not decided otherwise—and this is a mere concluding phrase, a reservation for safety's sake. Prosperity and riches are the goal. To achieve this goal, the young businessman must remember that time is money, that money well placed earns interest, that honesty and punctual repayment, like hard work, increase credit. It is ill-advised to be seen frequenting taverns, for it may frighten credit-givers: 'In short, the way to wealth, if you desire it, is as plain as the way to market. It depends chiefly on two words, industry and frugality; that is, waste neither time nor money, but make the best use of both.'[44]

This is the antithesis of the teachings to be found in such writers as Baxter, Penn, Fox, Wesley and Bunyan. They feared that the virtues which ought to be practised for religious reasons might lead to riches and felt it necessary to reduce the risks, or better still neutralise them, by sounding a warning against inordinate expansion of business, and by inducing the rich to give away their wealth. Franklin, and later writers such as Sumner,[45] do not regard diligence and thrift primarily as virtues in themselves but as a *means* of attaining wealth and getting on in the world. Franklin could have served as a model for the covetous man whose 'rational' attitude to virtue and piety as an expedient for getting rich caused Bunyan's true pilgrim to speak of Judas Iscariot and the depths of infamy.

For the sake of argument let us assume for a moment that this represents the genuine 'spirit of capitalism' and that Weber was wrong about Protestantism and Puritanism but right about Franklin. In that case two conclusions follow: 1) It is the contrasts with Puritanism that give Franklin's creed this content of 'capitalistic faith'; 2) this secularised capitalism, endeavouring to equate the expedients of good business with true virtue, was

44 *Writings of Benjamin Franklin,* Vol. II, pp. 370—2.
45 See below, pp. 71—6.

not unique to Franklin; he was not the only one or even the first. Long before Franklin, there were many writings, both in Catholic and Protestant countries, in which the same or similar ideals had been preached—as an element, not of religious education, but of the training of capable businessmen.

Perhaps the most important example of the latter is furnished by Jacques Savary, a French Catholic, whose book *Le parfait négociant*[46] was first published in 1675, and subsequently appeared in a long succession of editions that were widely distributed and heartily plagiarised by numerous other authors of various countries.

His intention, wrote Savary, was to provide young men embarking upon business life with the correct principles to enable them to conduct their enterprises in the most efficient manner and avoid the pitfalls that await the careless and ignorant. The profession of businessman, and of merchant particularly, is noble and useful. Savary extols it in terms that are at times lyrical, at times almost religious, in their impress: *'la nécessité et utilité du commerce'* are asserted by Savary with the same enthusiasm as by his countryman and fellow-believer, Jean Bodin, a good hundred years before. In no profession are a keen intellect and sound common sense so necessary as in that of the businessman. He who intends to become a businessman must start equipping himself for his profession at an early age; at seven or eight years old he should learn mathematics, the art of writing and modern languages such as Italian, Spanish and German. Classical languages, rhetoric and philosophy, on the other hand, do not matter so much. They are dismissed as lacking utility. It is not enough simply to improve his knowledge of merchandise, currency problems and the like. He must also learn how to deal with customers—how to be pleasant even if no business ensues—and for the sake of his credit and

---

[46] J. Savary, *Le parfait négociant ou Instruction générale pour ce qui regarde le commerce de toute sorte de marchandises, tant de France que des pays étrangers* (1675). See also H. Hauser, *op. cit.*, pp. 267—308.

reputation he must display a high moral standard and be upright and punctilious in his transactions.

Piety is another prerequisite of success: 'Godliness and the love of God are what apprentices, ought to have always before their eyes; without them, God will never bless their trade and they will never succeed in their enterprises.'[47] If possible, i.e., if business affairs do not prevent it, businessmen should go to Mass every day.

A large business is more dignified than a small one, wholesale trade more genteel than retail. Like nearly all other writers on the subject in most 'modern' countries of that time, Savary criticises the tendency of entrepreneurs to amass a fortune so as to be able to retire from business, or to bring up their sons to other vocations and to buy them into *la robe*—the bureaucratic *élite*. Enterprise demands a large supply of capital. Therefore as much wealth as possible should be created and ploughed back into business operations. Well-to-do persons—sleeping partners, for example—should, at any rate, see to it that capital remains at the disposal of enterprise, for the good of trade and for their own profit. It is large firms, *des grandes entreprises,* that are most urgently needed.

This, it is worth repeating, was from a Catholic writer in a Catholic country, a hundred years before Benjamin Franklin. He was of distinguished position: a rich merchant and an adviser of Colbert. Large editions of his writings were published. It would be unsafe to venture an opinion as to whether Savary produced such an impact that Frenchmen and others developed a greater propensity to engage in business—and to bring piety, the celebration of Mass, and business into association. But it defies comprehension why his influence should be regarded as less than that of the Puritan fathers, with their mistrust of riches and their precept of moderation not only in food and drink but in business too; and why Savary's outlook should be regarded as less 'capitalistic' and less productive of the 'spirit of capitalism' than that of the Puritan preachers.

[47] Savary, *op. cit.,* Hauser, *op. cit.,* p. 278.

It is possible to go further back in time than Savary and find the same line of thought as he and Franklin were later to propound. As a debating point against Weber, Sombart drew attention in *Der Bourgeois* to the Renaissance writer Leon Battisti Alberti, who in 1450 discussed the principles of 'holy housekeeping,' in a work whose general approach to diligence and thrift as economic virtues and to the 'rationalisation' of human activity as a whole would have given Franklin himself no ground for objection.[48]

Weber took up Sombart's criticism on this point in a note four pages long.[49] He hunts zealously for points of difference between Franklin and Alberti. Minor variations of phraseology, such as the fact that Alberti speaks of the management of wealth while Franklin refers to the employment of capital, are inflated to major importance even though two different languages and a time-gap of 300 years are involved. Alberti's references to the enjoyment of life, family honour and the value of good ancestry—ideas which, says Weber, Franklin would have repudiated as 'aristocratic grandiloquence'—are magnified into fundamental points of contrast. When Alberti asserts the advantages of a large-scale enterprise with low costs, Weber declares this the antithesis of Franklin's principle of strict budgeting: not to permit expenditure to exceed income. It is a fantastic argument, in two ways. Firstly, the difference between Alberti and Franklin is difficult to understand. Secondly, even if the 'difference' be accepted as real, then on any reasonable view it is Alberti's approach, not Franklin's, that is genuinely 'capitalistic' and 'rational'. For Alberti commends the large enterprise conducted on rational lines, while Franklin, says Weber, cuts his coat according to his cloth.

Despite strenuous efforts along these lines, in the end Weber was unable to deny that Alberti displayed some degree of that

---

[48] W. Sombart, *Der Bourgeois*, p. 136 ff. Alberti's *I libri della Famiglia*, edited by G. Mancini, was published in 1908.

[49] *Gesammelte Aufsätze*, p. 38 ff.

rationalism in economic affairs of which Franklin represented the ideal. He then took refuge in another sort of difference. How can one believe, he writes, that such an academic speculation could develop the same kind of life-transforming power as a religious faith? It cannot have been a decisive factor unless Alberti's work rapidly achieved the status of a classic; unless it accorded with the conceptions held by substantial groups among his contemporaries; and unless it represented, to use Weber's terminology, an already widely diffused 'capitalistic spirit'.

Weber's retaliatory note abounds with sophistries, distortions and circular arguments. It may suffice, by way of a summary of the foregoing, to bring out the following points: 1) that Alberti's rationalism is challenged, only to be declared un-challengeable shortly thereafter—though, by contrast with Franklin's, of no account in the affairs of men; 2) that crucial importance is attached to insignificant divergences of phraseology between Alberti and Franklin, while little weight is attributed to the similarities in the central theme which, considering the gap in time and environment, are very great; 3) that these divergences—which may be rightly or wrongly conceived by Weber—are freely interpreted 'capitalistically' for Franklin but 'non-capitalistically' for Alberti; 4) that the rational, capitalistic temper (which in one place is stated to occur only among the Puritans and in Franklin, while in another it is declared to occur in Alberti as well but to affect human conduct only with Puritanism and Franklin) is presumed to derive only from the unique religious factor. A period of over 300 years, and wholly different environments and climates of social opinion: these apparently play no role in the discrepancies alleged by Weber. Only Franklin's heritage of Puritanism is admitted in explanation of the fact that he expresses himself differently on a number of points from Alberti writing more than 300 years earlier.

This singular technique of emphasising the Puritan element in Franklin by finding differences where the most interesting and striking features seem to be the similarities is used by Weber in another case which he quotes.

On one occasion the ageing financial magnate, Jacob Fugger, was asked by a business friend why he did not, like the questioner himself, retire from business. Fugger, he said, had certainly earned more than enough and ought to be able, with an easy mind, to let someone else take over. Fugger replied that he had quite different ideas and intended to continue enlarging his fortune as long as he was capable.[50]

Werner Sombart judged this statement of Fugger's to be an expression of true capitalistic spirit. And in the first edition of *Der Moderne Kapitalismus,* he used Fugger's words as the motto of the chapter 'Die Genesis des modernen Kapitalismus'.

Weber, however, with whose theories such an interpretation was incompatible, declares that Fugger's statement reveals an approach which is 'manifestly' (*offensichtlich*) quite removed from that of Puritanism and Franklin. Fugger's approach, he writes,[51] was the morally neutral outlook of the merchant, while Franklin's was an ethically coloured principle of the conduct of life. Franklin, who early in life based his plans on being able to retire from business and devote himself to study and science, was thus more capitalistic, more single-mindedly dedicated to his profession, than the rich Jacob Fugger, in the evening of his life and still enthusiastically at work increasing his tremendous fortune![52]

The definition of the 'spirit of capitalism' which Weber is forced to construct when making these comparisons between Franklin on the one hand and Alberti and Fugger on the other

[50] On the Fuggers, see R. Ehrenberg, *Das Zeitalter der Fugger* (2 vols; 3rd Ed. 1922), esp. Vol. I, p. 118.

[51] Weber, *Gesammelte Aufsätze,* p. 33.

[52] In fact both Sombart's and Weber's interpretation of Jacob Fugger's statement are built on a misunderstanding. The story is derived from Ehrenberg's work, which originally appeared in 1896. There however it is not a question of Fugger's departure from the management of business affairs but simply of a withdrawal from hazardous enterprises in Hungary; to this suggestion Fugger replied, according to Ehrenberg, that 'er wolle gewinnen, so lange er könnte'. The story has thus been 'improved'.

is, to put it mildly, extraordinary. He is obliged to make no less than two complete circles. First the 'spirit of capitalism' is announced to be just that approach to economic activity which is principally displayed by the Reformed and Free church teachers and which reaches full maturity in Benjamin Franklin. Then, 'in proof' of this proposition, it is asserted that this spirit is to be found especially well developed in just those people. Next, diligence and thrift are declared to be the most vital elements in economic progress, and the 'rationalisation' of life and economic affairs the prime mover behind the economic success of the individual. Thereupon, diligence, thrift and a 'rational' approach to life are ascribed, without further proof, to economically successful groups in Protestant countries.

Even if we accept Weber's contention that a difference between the pre- and post-Reformation capitalist outlook really existed (and denoted something more than the different ways in which different periods expressed the same things) the consequence of this line of reasoning would still be very odd. For it would imply that capitalism was entirely possible even without the 'capitalistic spirit' in Weber's sense. Nations or groups could be economically successful and capable of achieving material progress if destitute of the 'spirit of capitalism' equally well as if generously endowed with it. The spirit would thus, at best, be able to explain only certain dissimilarities in the grasp and the declared aims of activity, not the total result. And if this is so, what happens to Weber's hypothesis?

At different times and in slightly varying ways, businessmen, like other people, have 'rationalised' their activities, *ex post facto*. They have sought motives where no motive existed, or seemly motives where those of which they were conscious were not fit for the public eye or even for their own. The mercantilists spoke glibly of the good of the state and the balance of trade when it was mainly a question of privileges and subsidies. The early liberals spoke of the power of selfish actions to create utility and happiness for all when it was chiefly a matter of getting rich. In our own day, the same activities as those of the mercantilists and early liberals are glorified by talk of welfare and a rising general standard of living, even though the immediate and primary aim is to avoid increased state intervention or higher wages. Calvinists, Puritans and others appointed the Almighty their chief public relations officer, as indeed have all religious movements.

None of these forms of 'rationalisation' was necessarily dishonest, deliberately mendacious or cynical. Those concerned may in every case have meant exactly what they said. But there is no practical difference worth mentioning if one nation or merchant grows rich by courtesy of a favourable balance of trade, another by the favour of God, and a third on the plea that only if man allows himself to be directed by the profit motive can he contribute to the felicitous evolution of society. While not in the least denying that in the world of economic ideas, just as much as in that of politics, culture or religion, new currents repeatedly asserted themselves, one cannot but agree with Sombart (his prodigious barrage of notions could hardly fail to hit the target now and then) in his contention that the essential difference in conduct and outlook between the Italian merchant classes of 'pre-capitalism' and the capitalists of Protestantism was slight. The essential qualities of eagerness to make money, to organise and expand firms, and to acquire power were held in common, no matter how these activities may have been justified in different centuries. We meet it in the successful merchants of the Italian Renaissance cities just as much as in the textile manufacturers and exporters of Catholic Flanders; in the Portuguese mercantile houses equally with the Puritan slave traders of 18th century New England or the financial barons of New York, Boston and Chicago in the late 19th and early 20th centuries.

4. THE CAPTAINS OF INDUSTRY

It is true that many of the industrialists and financiers of the United States in the late 19th and early 20th centuries were

Protestants, and indeed belonged to Calvinist and Puritan sects. It is also striking, as was last pointed out by Irwin G. Wyllie in 1954, to what extent clergymen or ex-clergymen appeared in 19th century America as eulogisers and apologists of the free economy, of capitalism and capitalists. Wyllie illustrates, involuntarily but excellently, how this observation can all too easly lead to Weberesque conclusions. Wyllie even finds that Weber is not sufficiently Weberian. By emphasising the strong secular element in Benjamin Franklin, says Wyllie, Weber retreats much too far from the basic concept of the importance of the religious influence. God and Mammon, he declares, were reconciled by those writers on economic subjects who were influenced by religion.[53]

Wyllie, however, quotes one or two vital facts which run directly counter to his thesis and indeed seem to make it quite untenable. All the well-known writers of what might be termed the 'capitalistically-religious' sort in 19th century America, e.g. John Todd, Matthew H. Smith, Francis E. Clark, Wilbur F. Crafts, H. Ward Beecher, Lyman Abbott, William Lawrence, William van Doren, Thomas Hunt, Russell Conwell, Daniel Wise and Horatio Alger, grew up, lived and worked in districts experiencing industrialisation and brisk economic growth. They were sons, cousins or friends of prominent businessmen. Their congregations and churches were largely dependent upon the donations of industrialists and merchants.

There was certainly no question, save in exceptional instances, of corrupted views in the ordinary sense. These writers were all exposed to what one may call the 'general influence of environment'. Industrialisation and business prosperity were seen to be beneficial to the communities in which they lived. The leaders of economic expansion were often God-fearing men, dutiful members of the church and economic pillars of their congregation. Was it not natural then to see economic activity as one aspect of God's work and the 'captains' of this activity as God's agents before others? It is surely no coincidence that,

[53] I. G. Wyllie, *op. cit.*, p. 56.

despite a deliberate search, Wyllie does not succeed in finding a single clergyman from the rural districts of America, from agricultural or lumbering regions, preaching the gospel of economic success. Industrialisation, economic growth, capitalism and capitalists were the 'primary' factors, their commendation in religious writings 'secondary'.

Naturally, the identification between God and Mammon made by these preachers was not without significance. It made a deep impress upon the outlook and idiom of many of the great financial barons of late 19th century America. But it was not the worship of God that led to the worship of Mammon. It was rather that it was felt necessary to demonstrate that devotion to wealth was not necessarily an impediment to true piety— *and the need to assert this was all the greater because so many of the Puritan fathers had so intensely feared the harmfulness of riches*. Religion had to revise its ideas, partly perhaps so as not to stand in the way of the economic transformation, but chiefly in order to keep up with the evolution that had been in rapid progress for some time, away from the world of small-scale agriculture and petit bourgeois craft industry towards a society marked by large-scale industry and world-wide trade. 'O ye Methodists, hear the word of the Lord. Who has believed our report? I fear: not many rich.' We may safely assume that these words of the father of Methodism were no longer regarded as socially acceptable in the America where power and social influence had begun to gravitate into the hands of the Vanderbilts and Rockefellers, Carnegies, Astors, their like.[54]

[54] On the American industrial leaders and the 'capitalist spirit,' see in general: R. G. McCloskey, *American Conservatism in the Age of Enterprise* (1951), esp. pp. 22—71; F. L. Allen, *The Big Change* (1952), p. 67 ff.; G. Harrison, *Road to the Right* (1954), pp. 162—74; Adams, *op. cit.*, p. 268 ff.; Wish, *op. cit.*, pp. 300 ff., 312 ff., c.f. also p. 177; Wyllie, *op. cit.*, p. 23 ff.; S. H. Holbrook, *The Age of the Moguls* (1954), pp. 88, 320, 346; A. Nevins, *Ordeal of the Union* (2 vols., 1947), *Ford, The Times, The Man, The Company* (1954), and *Study in Power. John D. Rockefeller, Industrialist and Philanthropist* (2 vols., 1953); J. D. Glover, *The Attack on Big Business* (1954), p. 139 ff.; C. A. Beard, *Economic Origins of Jeffersonian Democracy* (1949), p. 445 f.

The modification of religion made it possible for these industrial barons to be active members of various Protestant sects. It is true that religion, the observance of duty as a commandment of God, and the 'rationalisation' of economic activities by means of Bible quotations and sententious religious phrases, did exercise considerable influence on the speech, writings and general outlook of many of them; or at least that they were affected by a 'secularised' conception of a 'calling' approximating to that represented by Benjamin Franklin. But it is extremely uncertain how far all this reflected any really deep anchorage, so to speak, in these ideas, or how far it is justifiable to regard it as a force that motivated action. It is by no means necessary to postulate conscious dishonesty in order to ascribe some proportion of it to prevailing jargon rather than to deeply felt experience. In particular it should be borne in mind that the testimonies of their attitude to life and conduct bequeathed to us by members of this class of 'captains of industry,' e.g. Carnegie, Rockefeller and Ford, were written rather late in the day. They were written at the time of life when the activity of *ex post* rationalisation, and the urge to explain and defend tend to become pronounced. Such men do not say, and would rather not believe themselves, that all these riches are the result of fortunate coincidence, or uncommonly cynical transactions, or even simply of pure financial and organising genius. On the contrary, they speak of their hard struggle, of diligence and thrift, of high ideals, the fulfilment of their calling, their efforts to serve the common welfare, and similar niceties. Was it not in reality for these, my workers, that I have striven? Was it not the call of duty and the Almighty that I was answering when I triumphed in my affairs? Such notions yield an agreeable sensation and are easily believed by the questioner himself. And so, perhaps, Franklin and the Bible are invoked. Or Adam Smith. Or, to be more accurate, all the general, early liberal ideas on the efficacy of the profit motive and the promotion of the general welfare through the agency of free enterprise.

The 19th century sees the appearance in America—and not only in America—of a body of conservative-liberal ideas which, on the plea of the blessings of economic expansion, takes the field in defence of 'big business' against the vigorous attacks then being made upon it, and endeavours to justify *laissez-faire* and the entrepreneur's right to unrestricted freedom of action. These ideas, with their injunctions to respect the captains of industry, were derived from various system of thought, ranging from the early religious concept of the 'calling' and Franklin's later, secularised form of it to the liberal concept of utility and Darwin's theory of evolution by natural selection.

If any of the many ingredients in this confection of ideas about 'big business' at that time stands out more prominently than others, it is social Darwinism. The writings of Herbert Spencer were studied assiduously. From the end of the Civil War up to the turn of the century, over 350,000 copies of them were sold on the American market, and Spencer's visit to the United States in 1882 turned out to be a superbly triumphal progress. Within the United States, it was William Graham Sumner whose social Darwinism made him the chief ideological hero of the captains of industry.[55]

It may be said, of course, that some elements in this trend had affinities with religious ideas, with the ideals of Puritanism or of Protestantism generally. Such affinities can be traced between almost all 'ideologies'—between, let us say, early liberalism and Marxism—without it being supposed that the one was therefore the creator of the other. In essentials, social Darwinism as formulated by Sumner and others is different in kind from the system of opinion we are considering, e.g., Puritanism, Methodism and Quakerism, despite direct or indirect

[55] In his admirable work, *American Conservatism in the Age of Enterprise*, R. G. McCloskey devotes no less than 50 pages to Sumner out of a total of 170. A number of other works on American ideological currents and industrial expansion in the late 19th century draw attention to the significance of Sumner and/or social Darwinism. For Sumner's own views, see W. G. Sumner, *Folkways* (1906), *Earth-Hunger and Other Essays* (1913) and *What Social Classes owe to Each Other* (1920).

influence on a number of specific matters. Certain initial points of similarity—Sumner, like several of the writers mentioned above, began as a Calvinist priest, just as Luther and Calvin began as Catholics and Wesley as an Anglican—do not preclude the doctrine preached being in all vital respects a different one from its religious precursors. It is chiefly on the question of the attitude towards enterprise and wealth that the contrasts become evident.

In Sumner's view, capital and riches were 'the instrumentality by which, from the beginning, man has won and held every step of his development of civilization'.[56] To increase capital is therefore the highest social good. He who creates capital serves society in the only truly meaningful way. The objection that, even if this is true, the concentration into a few hands of great wealth and the monopolies associated therewith are dangerous, is countered by Sumner with an argument that is central to social Darwinism generally and Spencer in particular: it is the most able who survive the contest, and of these survivors it is those of supreme capacity who achieve the greatest success. Ability is identical with the capacity to contribute to economic progress. The idea of equality, which was of crucial importance to the Methodists and Quakers and was *one* of the reasons for their misgivings about riches, and their condemnation of business and the accumulation of capital beyond a certain quite modest level, is flatly rejected by Sumner: 'Let it be understood that we cannot go outside of this alternative: liberty, survival of the fittest; not liberty, equality, survival of the unfittest.'[57] The former principle impels society forward and favours the best citizens; the latter holds it back and favours the worst. It is true that uncontrolled free enterprise produces millionaires and monopolists. But this is by no means to be deplored. Great inequalities of income and fortune ought

[56] W. Sumner, *Earth-Hunger,* p. 341.
[57] W. Sumner, *The Challenge of Facts,* p. 25 (quoted McCloskey, *op. cit.,* p. 49).

not only to be tolerated; they ought to be encouraged by every possible means.

But it is not only the eulogising of riches, of the creation of wealth and of wide social distinctions that separates this spirit —'capitalistic' in very truth—from the Calvinistic type of religious outlook. In those paragraphs where Sumner, deliberately or not, reveals some remnants of the general moral conceptions he acquired during his period as a Puritan clergyman, he comes into direct collision with his enthusiasm for business enterprise. He has to admit that the existence of a powerful plutocracy may entail dangerous political consequences for democracy. But even though these tendencies ought to be resisted as far as possible, the evil must nevertheless be borne so that the community may reap the benefit of the blessings conferred by the wealthy classes in the form of progress and social welfare. Diligence and thrift are virtues. But they are not self-justifying as is asserted by such religious leaders as Wesley, Penn and Fox. They justify themselves only if they actively contribute to economic progress. Conversely, the successful entrepreneur in the full flood of success is just as valuable whether he practises such virtues or not.[58]

Sumner was the most reasoned and thoroughgoing literary spokesman for free enterprise and the 'spirit of capitalism' to accompany the American economic revolution, from the period of the Civil War up to and after the First World War. This does not mean that that spirit was the source and motivation of expansion and that we have in Sumner and social Darwinism what Weber thought he had found in Protestantism. For it was principally a matter of a thriving capitalism seeking and finding its champion and interpreter, not of impetus being imparted to capitalism through the preaching of its doctrines. Or, to echo McCloskey:[59] if Malthus and Darwin had not existed, the America of the 1870s would have had to invent them. But they did

[58] W. Sumner, *Folkways,* p. 40.
[59] McCloskey, *op. cit.,* p. 30.

exist; their gospel needed its St. Paul, and it found him in Sumner.

There were apostles at his side. In particular, the great entrepreneurs themselves adopted the doctrines and propagated them in more or less orthodox form. They made of them a variegated medley incorporating odds and ends from Malthus, Darwin, Spencer and Sumner, bits and pieces from Adam Smith and Benjamin Franklin, and the rest culled from sundry democratic, moral, philosophical and religious appraisements of one sort or another. Puritan and other Protestant concepts, and Catholic too, had a share in all this. To try to isolate the Protestant and Reformed church elements as they happen to fit in with the Weber hypothesis is an utterly hopeless task. And to see the captains of industry as exponents of the Protestant spirit is a simplification amounting to pure humbug.

Andrew Carnegie, with his *penchant* for giving both written and spoken vent to his thoughts on great sociological issues, furnishes us with the best view of how the 'spirit of capitalism' revealed itself in the industrial barons themselves.[60] He was probably not typical in every respect. By the very fact that he tried to formulate his ideas into a comprehensive philosophy he differed from the majority. But it may reasonably be assumed that on the whole the thoughts and feelings of his compeers, though less clearly systematized than his, found expression through him. McCloskey cites him as a man who 'in his life and his opinions exemplifies' the general characteristics of his age.[61] As will be shown later, similar ideas are to be discerned in Henry Ford and others.

It may be as well to stress first the strongly anti-religious bias of Carnegie. His father had broken with the Calvinist doctrine; his mother's family had long been emancipated from religious ties. He regarded with alarm such contacts with the religious

[60] I have drawn here on Carnegie's own *Triumphant Democracy* (1893), *The Empire of Business* (1902) and his *Autobiography* (1922). See also below, pp. 84—6.

[61] McCloskey, *op. cit.*, p. 134.

life of his Scottish homeland as he could not avoid: 'I well remember that the stern doctrines of Calvinism lay as a terrible nightmare upon me.'[62] His detestation and contempt for religious creeds came to form a trinity with his detestation and contempt for hereditary privilege and for monarchy. Of course, his taking up of this attitude does not necessarily imply that he was totally unaffected by the Calvinist outlook on life. Carnegie was by no means incapable of spiritual exercises. But, writes McCloskey: 'His cast of mind was too genial and optimistic to become entangled in the dour Presbyterian formulations.'[63] It is difficult to study Carnegie's autobiography without receiving the same impression.

The social philosophers most commonly invoked by Carnegie are Darwin and Spencer. According to his own account, he had read these with avid interest until he felt able to say: 'That settles the question.'[64] The most interesting point about Carnegie is that he felt, or at any rate recorded, a moral dilemma. He found himself—or made his writings indicate that he found himself—caught in the continual crossfire of incompatible ideals. The demand for equality, democracy, and the right of labour to use the strike weapon in fighting for better conditions were difficult to reconcile with the unrestrained heaping-up of wealth and the furious speculations of the few—in short, complete *laissez-faire*. Up to a point, Carnegie contrived to bridge these contradictions tolerably well. Equality became equality of opportunity to get on in the world, the right of every individual to climb to the summit of affluence and society, unimpeded by hereditary privilege. Viewed in this light, to be born poor was held to be an asset; indeed, a childhood spent in poverty was virtually suggested to be a condition of success. Without poverty, men of outstanding ability could not be produced, and without such men progress was impossible: 'Abolish luxury, if you please, but leave us the soil, upon which alone the virtues

[62] Carnegie, *Autobiography*, p. 22.
[63] McCloskey, *op. cit.*, p. 139.
[64] *Ibid.*, p. 138.

and all that is precious in human character grow: poverty—
honest poverty.'[65]

On some points, however, the gulf between contending ideals
proves more difficult to spirit out of existence. In such cases,
the conflict is resolved in favour of economic progress. To the
accompaniment of mental qualms more painful than those of
Sumner, who indeed seems to have been quite untroubled by such
embarrassment, Carnegie comes to the same conclusions as does
Sumner. In the end, the victory always goes to the relentless
quest for wealth. Wherever the general claims of democracy
seem inconsistent with 'progress' they are forced to surrender to
the conviction that the wealth of Carnegie and his kind has a
deeper social purpose, and that in the long run democracy will
best benefit if he and his business friends are left alone. Thus
were capitalism and democracy harmonised. Democracy serves
the ends of capitalism and makes the capitalist system possible
through the freedom it gives to the able. Capitalism repays the
debt by enriching and elevating democracy.

In the end democracy becomes equal voting rights and nominally equal opportunity for all. The privileges and power
created by wealth are an inevitable consequence of democracy
and the survival of the fittest. Carnegie's book *Triumphant
Democracy*, which purports to constitute a defence of democracy,
turns out to be an apologia for industrial capitalism as manifested in the United States of the late 19th century, and for
Carnegie himself and his like. It is possible that some twinge
of bad or at least uneasy conscience actuated the author, and
that he felt called upon to vindicate his business conduct and
his prodigious wealth before the public and himself. At all
events, the result was entirely satisfactory to less sensitive souls—
i.e., to most of his compeers.

Henry Ford's approach differs in one respect.[66] Ford despised
mere financiers. He was a provincial manufacturer on a gigantic

[65] *Empire of Business,* p. 129.

[66] For Ford's view I have used his *My Life and Work* (1922) and

scale, and possessed that direct predilection of the production executive for drawing an impassable frontier between 'finance' and 'production'. But this eccentricity apart, his general outlook is like Carnegie's, though simpler. Progress and economic expansion are all that matter; they are ends in themselves. If these ends are to be achieved, then enterprise, even in the forms detested or despised by Ford, must have its head:

'Business is merely work. Speculation in things already produced—that is not business. It is more or less respectable graft. But it cannot be legislated out of existence. Laws can do very little. Law never does anything constructive. It can never be more than a policeman, and so it is waste of time to look to our state capitals or to Washington to do that which law was not designed to do. As long as we look to legislation to cure poverty or to abolish special privilege we are going to see poverty spread and privilege grow.'[67]

And he sums up: 'We can help the Government: the Government cannot help us.'[68]

The same theme is repeated elsewhere. Only free enterprise can supply humanity's needs:

'The world has been baffled by poverty. Sometimes it has been so baffled that it has made a virtue of poverty, and men have set up that they were proud to be poor. The only escape from poverty was held out by religion promising Heaven as a surcease from sorrow'...[69]

He who makes the best goods, whose designs and production processes are so well conceived that people want only his mer-

Today and Tomorrow (1926) (both written in collaboration with Samuel Crowther). In this context of Ford and Carnegie I see no reason to refer here to the mass of 'muck-raking' literature; and a critical analysis of source material would be altogether too long.

[67] Life and Work, p. 7.
[68] Ibid.
[69] Today and Tomorrow, p. 265.

chandise, is said to show 'sound business sense'. But that is not all: 'that is morality.'[70] He who produces most efficiently what people want to buy is the most able and will achieve the greatest success. Therefore he who is most able is best for the community at large. The process of selection is so rational that not even monopoly is to be feared. 'The only monopoly possible is based upon rendering the highest service. That sort of monopoly is a benefit.'[71]

Material progress as the great objective and the fundamental driving force is Ford's doctrine. In this he goes even further, if that is possible, than Carnegie. The latter was aware of spiritual values, of art, literature, philosophy and culture generally. Ford despised books, did not understand art and indeed never bothered his head about 'what people need' beyond material things—house and home, food and cars.

Between the philosophy of Sumner, Carnegie and Ford and the view of economic activity as a means of winning salvation and the grace of God, ascribed by Max Weber to Calvinism and the Calvinist sects, there is an abyss.

The wholly secularised Carnegie, abjurer of Christian doctrine; the warmly religious Rockefeller; the nominally Protestant Jim Hill, whose largest donations went to Catholic institutions; John Jacob Astor and Cornelius Vanderbilt, to whom religious speculations were plainly unfamiliar; Ford the simple provincial: in all of them we find this singular and mongrel ideology. From a variety of philosophies they picked out whatever contributed to the defence of their own conduct, riches and power. Whether it was God or Franklin or some more generalised conception that was invoked, this ideological farrago stands revealed—insofar as it bears scrutiny at all—as a rationalisation of accomplished facts rather than a motivating force. To put it more specifically: John Jacob Astor did not have God or his 'calling' in mind when he set on foot the

[70] *Ibid.*, p. 268.
[71] *Ibid.*, p. 21.

speculation and lawsuits that diverted into his pockets the enormous profits accruing from the appreciation of land values in New York State; nor did Cornelius Vanderbilt when, buccaneer-like, he was laying the foundations of his business empire; nor did Ford when he designed the Model T; nor Eli Whitney when interchangeable spare parts were invented; nor David Drew, Jay Gould or Jim Fisk when dealing in gold and securities; nor Rockefeller when conquering competitors and buying up other firms; nor Carnegie when venturing upon his early speculations. The ideologies were not launched until later, when *faits accomplis* were being explained and defended.

5. SUMMARY

To summarise. The 'spirit of capitalism' which we have found in Benjamin Franklin and the captains of industry, as well as in such figures as Alberti, Fugger and Savary, did not flow from Puritanism and its teachings, but on the contrary was different in kind from these teachings. The self-same element which, on any reasonable view, constituted the 'capitalistic' component and 'economic' approach to life in Franklin and the great pioneers of the late 19th and early 20th centuries, was the feature that principally distinguished their views from Puritanism. In their general attitude to economic problems, the great Puritan teachers, with their mistrust of riches and the temptations of this world, were anything but capitalistically inclined.

Although we seem to have established that Weber's and Tawney's estimate of the significance of the predestination concept was mistaken, it has become apparent at various points in the foregoing that Puritanism unquestionably encouraged diligence and thrift (in the sense of low standards of consumption among individuals). Some indications have also been found that the attitude of Calvinism to the problem of usury may have diverged from that of Catholicism. Is it justifiable on these bases to infer that the Reformed church doctrines produced an 'indirect' effect upon economic life, as has been suggested in particular by Tawney and Ashley?

This question can only be answered by analysing the content of the doctrines themselves. Indeed, two further questions must be asked as well. Firstly: was Puritanism's recorded attitude to diligence, thrift and free interest rates something unique to this form of religion, or did it merely reflect patterns of thought generally accepted by the age? Secondly: what influence did diligence, thrift and higher or lower interest rates have on economic trends? Can they have formed at least some part of the foundation of capitalism?

CHAPTER III

Virtue, Interest and Wealth

1. DILIGENCE AND THRIFT

The doctrine of diligence and thrift that was preached to mankind for three centuries—roughly the 16th, 17th and 18th—was not unique to Protestantism, Calvinism and the free religious sects. It constituted a most important feature of the moral outlook of mercantilism, which everywhere reigned supreme. It was preached in Catholic France with the same zeal as in Switzerland and the Netherlands.

Idleness and luxury were the great vices. Scarcely a single mercantilist writer or politician failed to emphasise the point. In England, some time before the Reformation, the abominableness of 'idle and unprofitable' persons was vigorously proclaimed, and a number of 16th and 17th century writings free of all religious bias single out idleness as the 'root of all evil,' or the 'foundation of all those vices which prevail amongst us,' or are concerned lest it should 'suck the breasts of industry'. The abhorrence of idleness was even stronger in France, where this iniquitous phenomenon was most energically scourged. Idleness was 'the grave of living men'. In the matter of urging his subjects to diligence and thrift, Colbert was more ardent even than Calvin himself. Child labour—often starting at the age of six—was decreed because 'experience has always certainly shown that idleness in the first years of a child's life is the real source of all the disorders in later life'.[1] This corresponds practically word for word with the view expressed by Wesley, and everywhere in vogue. It was, too, such universally held opinions that Cunningham, when he found them in Scotland, viewed as peculiarly Puritanical. In fact, the child labour in Scotland that Cunningham regarded as proof of Presbyterianism's ethos of toil was practised with the same severity and on exactly the some grounds in Catholic France. In 1668, Colbert prescribed that in certain of the textile districts children should begin manufacturing work at the age of six so as to escape the perils of youthful idleness.[2]

Luxury also was pilloried everywhere, at any rate when it manifested itself in circles other than the court and higher nobility or when not of direct importance as a sales outlet for native industries. When luxury produced utility in this latter way, it was unhesitatingly applauded, by Franklin for example. But otherwise, luxury and extravagance were harmful. Everywhere, merchants and manufacturers were sharply criticised on the ground that they neither worked nor saved hard enough, and that they perpetually resorted to credit instead of creating the capital they needed out of their own resources.

These attacks can, of course, be variously interpreted. The very zeal of the preachers may be seen as a sign that the virtues of diligence and thrift were more praised than practised. Why emphasise so assiduously qualities universally present among the people? Or, leaving aside Weber's erroneous interpretation of the meaning of the doctrine of predestination, it may be suggested that there was a difference between, on the one hand, the effect produced by mercantilism's 'utility doctrine,' with its stress on the secular, and on the other, a religious conception that spiritual welfare was involved as well as temporal, indeed that temporal welfare was an index of the spiritual eternity awaiting the diligent and thrifty. There may be some truth in

[1] For these quotations, see Heckscher, *Mercantilism,* Vol. II, pp. 154—5.
[2] *Ibid.,* p. 156.

such hypotheses. Perhaps Colbert thundered so loudly because his rules were not being followed. Perhaps Calvin, aided by the power of religious faith and fanaticism, penetrated the roots of the soul more deeply and secured the translation of these injunctions into action.

But how far were they translated into action? To what extent were diligence and thrift virtues that were practised in one place more than in another? And to what extent did they contribute to economic progress? No clear and unequivocal answer can be given. This absence of an answer is sufficient in itself. For as long as these questions cannot be answered, then at all events Weber's theory remains uncorroborated. Not only the influence of diligence and thrift upon economic progress but the very existence of these qualities must be substantiated if the Weberian correlation between them and Protestant doctrine is to bear any kind of meaning.

Even though a clear answer remains out of the question, there are, nevertheless, two relevant points which can be established.

Firstly, it is quite evident that, with few exceptions, those persons and classes in the most economically advanced countries who were the main representatives of the kind of economic activity relevant to the present purpose were not characterised by thrift in its strict Puritan or ascetic sense. It is true that contemporary complaints about the extravagant way of life of big merchants, manufacturers or ironmasters were exaggerated in the sense that such complaints overlooked the element of 'competitive consumption,' the essential business entertainment, the improvement of creditworthiness and enhancement of social standing that were contained in a high style of life. It is also true that the ratio of these costs to the total was greatly over-estimated. This does not prevent the details recorded often being correct in themselves.[3] Practical reality was as far removed

[3] On 'competitive consumption,' see K. Samuelsson, *De stora köpmans-husen i Stockholm 1730—1815. En studie i den svenska handelskapitalis-mens historia* (1951), p. 220 f., and K.-G. Hildebrand, 'Monopolistisk konkurrens som ekonomiskt-historiskt problem,' *Ekonomisk Tidskrift* (1951).

from the frugality enjoined by Calvinism and Puritanism as it was possible to be. The palatial old residences of businessmen in one mercantile city after another—Berne, Geneva, Zürich, Amsterdam, Antwerp, London, Lübeck, Danzig, Stockholm—are testimony enough. Summer residences, country estates and pleasure yachts, records of servants, vehicles, clothes, funerals, weddings and other festivals complete the picture. A way of life verging on the lavish was far more typical than the pathological niggardliness that Calvin, Colbert and the Free church fathers all exalted as the ideal.

Rockefeller and Carnegie are often instanced as examples of an almost morbid thriftiness. Yet the effective role of this trait—when it existed at all—was surely negligible. The great palaces, the princely courts with which such seigneurs surrounded themselves must not be obscured by the vision of the frugal meals or turned suits they may have affected. Many great capitalists have taken pleasure or snobbish pride in a certain personal simplicity, in economy over trivalities; and this has often duped both contemporaries and posterity. People note and magnify the image of a Rockefeller or a Morgan holding a glass of milk. In the popular image, should not such men drink champagne every morning? Or of a Carnegie in a turned suit. Surely a legendary figure in sables, his fingers glittering with precious stones?

Secondly, the whole concept of an intimate association between thrift and the large-scale accumulation of capital is doubtful. Obviously thrift and diligence were often a prerequisite of a successful start in life: the capital saved by parents or relatives, hard years of self-denial to secure sufficient education, to perfect an invention, to get an idea successfully launched, or to scrape up a little capital to branch out independently. Swedish industrial entrepreneurs, for example, seem usually to have followed moderate, if not exactly frugal, habits of life during the early years when they were establishing themselves. But standard rose as incomes rose, and among the fairly prosperous the standard of living seems generally to have been at a level appropriate to the upper class of the period. And thrift as a virtue of necessity rather than a virtue in itself is *not* what Weber meant, but the very antithesis of this.

Nor can thrift have been the principal means of amassing such concentrations of capital as the enormous fortunes of the great manufacturers and merchants in England and the Netherlands. The possession of great wealth and the command of really important capital assets—and this is what we must consider, not the painfully hoarded coppers of small traders and craftsmen— can scarcely have derived, even exceptionally, from 'saving up' in the connotation usually implied by this expression, a connotation which Weber must also have intended if his argument is to make any sense at all. Although hard work has certainly and often made its contribution, great fortunes are, and for the most part always have been, the product of 'fortunate speculations,' of vast profits from vast risks and vast luck—in short, of speculation and capital gains usually in association with extensive structural changes and innovations in economic life.

Except in one or two instances during the modest early days, it was certainly not thrift that, in Sweden, brought riches to the Arfwedsons, Grills, Lefebures and Jennings, or later on to Wingquist, the Wallenbergs, the Johnsons and Wenner-Gren; nor was it thrift that made millionaires and multi-millionaires of the De Neufvilles, Hopes, Cliffords and Hogguers in 18th century Holland, or of Morgan, Carnegie, Rockefeller, Vanderbilt and Harriman in 19th century America. The determining factors were the volume and fortune of business, enormous capital gains on unexploited, or previously ill-exploited, natural assets, and the monopolisation of markets or credit.

With few exceptions, all great fortunes, far-flung economic empires and individual concentrations of economic power have been built up at tremendous speed, in the course of a single generation, not of two or three (although time may have increased wealth still further), in a single decade or even a single year. As W. W. Jennings points out when discussing the great American fortunes, it needs no very advanced mathematics to demonstrate that thrift cannot have been the explanation of the wealth of such as Carnegie or Rockefeller.[4] If Carnegie had saved 10,000 dollars a year he would have needed 4,500 years to reach 45 million dollars, i.e., he would have had to start at about the time that the pyramid of Cheops was built. It would not be proper to assume compound interest on the capital sums over this long period, because of course Carnegie only had a few decades at his disposal. When he retired, it was with a personal fortune of 375 million dollars. If John D. Rockefeller, who was estimated in 1921 to possess three thousand million dollars, had saved 100,000 dollars a year, he would have needed 30,000 years. At this time (1921) fifty American families had fortunes of over 100 million dollars each and a hundred families over 50 million dollars each. Let us take another example. Anyone who bought 20,000 dollars' worth of shares in General Motors in 1913 would have been worth about 15 million dollars in 1957. At 5 % compound interest, it would need an annual saving of 200,000 dollars for at least 30 years to reach a like amount. 'No man,' Jennings sums up, 'can legitimately save millions in a lifetime.'[5] Genius, sheer luck, a clear eye for market opportunities, a flair for publicity, hard work, low cunning, vast capital gains on natural assets—all these are possible and plausible factors. But to speak of thrift as a decisive or even substantial factor where large fortunes are concerned is utter nonsense.

[4] W. W. Jennings, *A History of Economic Progress in the United States* (1926), p. 739 f.

In general on the rise of the great fortunes, see R. Ehrenberg, *Grosse Vermögen, ihre Entstehung und ihre Bedeutung* (2 vols., 1902), on the Fuggers, Rotschilds, Krupps and Parishs; and B. C. Forbes, *Men who are making America* (1922). Of the fifty great industrialists and bankers whose varying careers are described in Forbes' book, at least forty became millionaires in some few years time. Cf. also Holbrook, *op. cit.; Fortunes made in Business* (various authors) (2 vols., 1884); T. W. Lawson, *Frenzied Finance* (1906); T. Gårdlund, *Svensk industrifinansiering under genombrottsskedet 1830—1913* (1947), and *Det goda livet* (1952), p. 132 ff., and esp. p. 138; C. W. Mills, *The Power Élite* (1956), p. 109 ff.

[5] Jennings, *op. cit.*, p. 739.

For a purpose quite different from that of this book Frederick Lewis Allen analysed a series of Horatio Alger's stories to see how the hero won his riches.[6] Alger is one of the group of writers, religiously inclined and preaching thrift and diligence, cited by Wyllie and others; he is generally considered to have exerted a tremendous influence on the American sense of values. The hero of Alger's books was always a poor boy who finished up rich. His first steps on the road to success were invariably marked by the twin virtues of diligence and thrift. This much is in harmony with the Weber theory. But at the crucial point, this harmony vanishes. To have the little lad reach the higher realms of wealth simply through diligence and thrift was straining credulity much too far even in moralistic stories for young people. In the end, Alger always resorted to a gigantic inheritance, left to his hero by some previously unknown relative, or as a gift from a multi-millionaire who felt the virtuous boy to be worthy of a reward. Thrift and diligence were adequate instruments for winning the favour of rich relatives or bosses or millionaires' daughters, but not for achieving wealth single-handed. Alger understood, and appreciated that his young readers would also understand, something that had evidently never occurred to Weber: in the real world, capital formation by individuals, the accumulation of large fortunes, and the concentration of economic power all occur through a variety of different media, and virtuous work and assiduous saving are clearly among the less usual and less effective of these.

2. HIGH AND LOW INTEREST RATES

Along with diligence and thrift, the doctrinal approach of the Reformed church to the problem of interest has figured prominently in the theories of Protestantism's contribution to economic growth. In the long chapter of his *Introduction to Economic History and Theory* which he intitled 'The Canonist

[6] F. L. Allen, *op. cit.*, pp. 69—70.

Doctrine,' Ashley shifted the whole emphasis of the argument to this aspect.[7] Just as Weber postulated a clear distinction between Luther's and Calvin's conception of the 'calling,' so did Ashley do the same for the charging of interest. Luther retained the Catholic approach to interest; Calvin, following the precedent of Melanchthon, jettisoned the view that the exaction of interest was wicked. Thus did Calvinism and not Lutheranism become capitalistic.

These conclusions are clearly contradicted by the evidence adduced by Ashley himself. If interest is regarded as the vital factor, this lends plausibility to the contentions of Sombart (in *Der Bourgeois*) and Robertson, that the new economic spirit was generated within Catholicism. It is true that, at the time of the Reformation, Catholicism still preserved in principle its negative attitude to the exaction of interest. The view that the practice was iniquitous can be traced back to Aristotle—and even to Moses, who forbade the exaction of interest from anyone except 'strangers,' i.e., foreigners. But in fact, Catholicism relaxed its ban on interest in one department of life after another. It became an ethical rule from which all deviations necessary to practical life were permitted.

It was over the question of borrowing by landowners that the dogmatic ban on interest was first lifted. Here, dogma clashed ever more sharply with reality. Landowners receiving 'interest' (rent) from their tenants regarded it as a right that could be sold like other rights. The difficulty of having the tenant pay his dues to a third party other than the proprietor of the land could be overcome. The landowner sold a piece of land, including the right to the rental, for a sum of money. Immediately thereafter, the property was returned to him, en-

[7] Ashley, *op. cit.*, pp. 377—488. See also Heckscher, *Mercantilism*, esp. Vol. II, p. 286. ('The canonical authorities had certainly tried, with adroitness and skill, to formulate the prohibition against interest in such a manner as not to collide more than necessary with economic activity, which indeed was inescapable.'); F. B. Artz, *The Mind of the Middle Ages, A. D. 200—1500. A Historical Survey* (1953), pp. 275 ff., 291 ff.; J. Schumpeter, *A History of Economic Analysis* (1954), p. 64 ff.

cumbered with the obligation to pay the rent on it. Nominally, a title to rent had been transferred; actually, the landowner had borrowed money as interest. From this it was but a short step to the assignment of rental rights at a single stroke, and from the latter in turn to the encumbering of the estate as a whole, not merely a certain portion of it, with interest charges in return for a cash loan. In the later Middle Ages, in fact, the lending of money at interest to owners of large estates was a normal investment outlet for liquid capital.

The ban on interest was also circumvented in another way. Even if it was thought improper to exact remuneration for the loan itself, there still remained the right to require compensation for damages sustained through the borrower neglecting his repayments. The ancient custom of delivering defaulting borrowers in servitude to the lender was revived, though in a less disagreeable form. They were sentenced to pay interest. It was also possible to insure beforehand against the likely defalcation of the borrower. Interest could be paid as an 'interest' in a different sense, i.e., a payment not for the loan itself but for the damages which it could be calculated beforehand would be suffered by the lender. Thus was the road to the exaction of interest cleared, even from the moralistic standpoint of the canonists. For except on paper, it was plainly impossible to devise any difference of status between pre-estimated damages on loans and the actual extent of monetary deprivation suffered by a lender over the period of the loan. In reality, the ban on interest did not imply more than a moral reflection, even with Aristotle; for he knew full well that the taking of interest on loans of money was practised and was bound to be practised.

There was another more important method, however; and here the association between the exaction of interest and non-agricultural forms of enterprise may explain why a connection between religious views on interest and the rise of capitalism has been so eagerly sought. In the commercial world, interest had to be permitted because the boundaries between ownership—part or sole—and investment at interest were impossible to define. Where was the line to be drawn between a merchant fitting out, though not participating in, a commercial expedition the leadership of which is wholly entrusted to an employed sea-captain, another merchant who joins with the captain in supplying the capital for the expedition, and a third who makes a loan to a captain who in essentials is mobilising the necessary capital himself? In the first two cases, the right to a return over and above the sum contributed to the adventure—i.e., to receive interest on it—was undisputed by canonical opinion. The third case was highly dubious, but in practice it was impossible to enforce any ban.

The ban on interest received its moral death blow from the Franciscans at the end of the 15th century. Beginning at Orvieto in 1463, they established benevolent funds for loans to the poor. In order to cover administrative costs, they charged a certain interest on their loans. The opposition aroused by the idea of a Catholic order exacting interest from those in the greatest need—the loudest protests came from the Dominicans—was parried by a strictly practical argument. If interest-free loans were the best of all, then loans from charitable funds at low interest were better than the high interest rates of professional money-lenders. Loans absolutely free of charge were simply not to be had. The Lateran Council of 1515 accepted this reasoning.

Thus, the 'new' view of interest had already emerged in practice by the time of the Reformation. The Calvinist outlook does not, as supposed by Weber and Ashley, constitute any explanation of capitalism—or at least not of this particular facet of it. Calvin's approach did not differ from that of many Catholic writers. It is true that, after lengthy deliberation and much hesitation, he did declare that the exaction of interest was not forbidden in all cases, and that it was a mere verbal exercise to make any distinction of principle between interest upon monetary loans and other forms of interest that were accepted universally, even by the Catholic church. But the fact that the exaction of interest was not forbidden in all cases did not imply freedom from all restrictions. Numerous conditions were imposed. Usurious battening upon distress was prohibited; nor was it permissib e to demand security in excess of what the poor man could bear. It was forbidden to charge interest on a loan unless the transaction could be reckoned likely to profit the borrower at least as much as the lender. It was further forbidden to charge higher rates of interest than the civil laws of the community allowed; and the fact that the exaction of interest was customary did not in principle signify that it was right. The terms and conditions of the contract in each specific case would decide the extent to which it conformed to these precepts. Prudence was called for; better to take too little than too much. Calvin declares that he experienced doubt and uneasiness. There is no authority in the Bible for an absolute and unconditional ban on interest. But is it not dangerous to say so, and will not men abuse a right that is not totally denied them?[8]

This is not to say, however, that the modifications of the Catholic outlook were decisive and that the 'pre-capitalism' theory on the influence of interest, as put forward by Cunningham, Sombart and Robertson, is correct. It is possible indeed that any discussion basing itself on opinions about legal statutes touching interest and enterprise is quite beside the point. Economic practice may well have gone its own way and followed its own 'laws' untroubled by canonical or Calvinist ideas of justice. There is undoubtedly ample warrant for Brentano's reference to the importance of Roman law in the sphere of practical life. The modifications of religious outlook (whether construed as having taken place within the framework of Catholicism or through the medium of the Reformation) did not in that case signify the creation of any new liberty.

On the contrary, these modifications could equally have expressed a reluctant recognition that liberation was an accomplished fact, just as the severity of the earlier statutes may have

[8] On Calvin and the interest problem, see Hauser, *op. cit.*, p. 45 ff., section entitled, 'Les idées économiques de Calvin'. On the mercantilists and interest, see Heckscher, *Mercantilism,* Vol. II, pp. 199 ff., 285 ff.

been due to the actual level of interest rates nearly always being so high that it was felt necessary to do something about them. Some indication that this may have been so is afforded by the stern insistence of the strictly Catholic Spanish regime that interest must not exceed 12 (*sic!*) per cent. The process by which the ban on interest was dissolved may have been analogous to that which can be observed in our own day in the realm of sexual behaviour. 'Relaxations' of ethical standards and the professed 'moral' outlook of society and individuals do not *precede* but *follow* changes in habits—or result from the discovery that habits, though perhaps almost unchanged, are quite at variance with 'public' opinion.

When, therefore, such writers as Robertson and Cunningham and in practice Ashley as well, stressed in certain connections the impact of political and economic changes upon the attitude to economic problems adopted by the religious creeds, they were attacking the problem from a promising angle. Yet in so doing, they themselves reveal that the enthusiasm with which they otherwise discuss the influence of religious faith on the ethical view of interest is misplaced. In fact, it seems clear that Calvin, who at heart was not really much interested in such matters, did not *create* a 'capitalistic spirit' when, after prolonged hesitation, he delivered a positive but far from lucid verdict on the interest problem. But he won the applause of business circles in the important mercantile city of Geneva, of those who were already exceedingly well endowed with the 'capitalistic spirit'; indeed, it was consciousness of these circles that wrung his declaration from him.

In discussing the problem of interest, another consideration should be borne in mind; it is one that casts serious doubt upon the form taken by the discussion about interest prohibitions and the fixing of maximum rates. Did free interest rates have anything to do with economic progress at all?

In the first place, it is clear that the rise of capitalism, that is to say in short the growth of capital mobilisation and credit provision on a large scale, was associated with a trend towards *lower* rates of interest, not *higher*. It was the shortage of liquid capital and the difficulty of obtaining credit that chased interest rates upwards. As soon as the mobilisation and lending of capital on a large scale came into being—and by definition they grew with 'capitalism'—interest rates fell. It was, *inter alia,* their observation of this fact that impelled a number of mercantilist writers, to whom money and capital were synonymous concepts, to plead that 'plenty of money decreaseth usury in price or rate,' and conversely that low interest rates promoted economic progress.[9] Two diametrically opposite conclusions concerning the fixing of maximum rates of interest might be drawn from these premisses. A 'ceiling' on interest rates might be advocated on the ground that low rates of interest seemed to be linked with economic progress. Or the statutory fixing of rates might be resisted on the ground of superfluity, since an increase in the supply of money (which was regarded as being identical with economic expansion) would of itself depress interest rates.

The most notable example of an association between economic progress and low interest rates was the Netherlands.[10] At the beginning of the 18th century, the rate of interest on securities listed on the stock exchanges of that country was down to 2 % and occasionally even 1¾ %. Extensive lending to other countries in the form of credits to trade and industry and the purchase of government securities—principally English, French, German and Austrian but including some Swedish as well—caused the rate of interest to rise eventually to between 3 and 5 %, a level substantially lower than the 5 and 6 %, prescribed by law in some places.

In the second place, it is by no means axiomatic that the

[9] Heckscher, *Mercantilism,* Vol. II, p. 200.
[10] See E. Baasch, *Holländische Wirtschaftsgeschichte* (1927), p. 194 ff.; Ehrenberg, *Das Zeitalter der Fugger,* Vol. II, p. 299 ff.; L. H. Jenks, *The Migration of British Capital to 1875* (1927), p. 7; C. Wilson, *Anglo-Dutch Commerce and Finance in the Eighteenth Century* (1941), p. 88; J. B. Manger, *Récherches sur les relations économiques entre la France et la Hollande pendant la revolution française* (1923), p. 60 ff. and *passim.*

association between economic progress and low rates of interest was one-sided in its operation and that it was invariably the latter that depended upon the former. As a number of mercantilists pointed out, the reverse process is also apparent. Low rates of interest exerted a stimulating influence on enterprise, trade and industry, because they made real investments more attractive than purely financial transactions. They increased the differential between entrepreneurial profit on the one hand and, on the other, the interest yield on such investments as government securities and the interest burden on borrowed capital. It is this relationship that Ashton stresses in connection with industrial expansion in 18th century England:

'The lower the rate at which capital could be obtained—the smaller the advantage forgone in locking it up in a fixed form—the further would capital works be extended ...... The deep mines, solidly built factories, well constructed canals, and substantial houses of the industrial revolution were the products of relatively cheap capital.'[11]

The rise of capitalism, particularly industrial capitalism, was associated not with higher interest rates, but with lower. Traditional Catholic opinion was at one with many Puritan writers in regarding interest, at all events when it was fairly high, as a moral evil. However, this did not imply that interest was not charged in practice, nor even, perhaps, that interest rates were normally lower than what way be described as the 'market level'. The mercantilists were little concerned with moral considerations. They wanted low interest rates for strictly economic reasons. Whether their agitation for an interest ceiling had any more effect than that of the Catholics it is impossible to determine. For our purposes, however, it will suffice to say this much: to the extent that the objective was achieved, without going so far as to wipe out the interest-differentials that attracted imports of capital from countries better endowed with

[11] Ashton, *Industrial Revolution*, pp. 10—11, cf. pp. 58, 82 and 91.

it, this policy constituted an encouragement, not a hindrance, to investment in plant and machinery, in ships and merchandise. Thus on the whole and in the long run it nourished economic progress. Therefore—and aside from the accuracy or inaccuracy of the interpretation placed upon the attitude of the various creeds to interest, and upon the impact of these attitudes on the situation actually prevailing in relation to interest at different points in time—the discussion of Catholic and Reformation attitudes to interest is in this vital respect founded upon an erroneous conception of the part played by interest in the development generally characterised as capitalistic.

CHAPTER IV

Correlations and Concepts

1. CORRELATIONS AND CAUSALITY

The starting point for Weber's assumption that a causal connection existed between Protestantism and economic progress consisted of two observations. The first was that in states of mixed religious faith, it was Protestants, and in wholly Protestant states the Puritan sects, who achieved particular economic success, and that in these groups there was a greater tendency than among the population at large to engage in trades and pursuits especially contributing to capitalist expansion. The second was that after the Reformation economic progress was particularly marked in Protestant countries, and that as between these latter it was more marked in Calvinist than in Lutheran-Evangelist countries.

How far were these assertions justified by the facts? Before attempting to answer this question, one or two general points must be made. It is evident that even if a correlation in strictly general terms can be said to have existed between forms of religious faith and economic progress, it does not necessarily follow that its nature was precisely as supposed by Weber, that religion generated economic progress. The relationship may equally well have been the converse one of prosperous countries becoming Protestant. It may even have been that certain countries—and certain sectors of the population within those countries—were at once Protestant and prosperous without these two facts having anything directly to do with one another; economic progress and the spread of Protestantism could each respectively have 'derived' from a third extraneous factor—or a combination of such extraneous factors.

The first of these alternatives, the idea that prosperous countries became Protestant, that a relationship existed but was the reverse of that suggested by Weber—found its leading advocate in Robertson. Although not formulated in explicit terms, the same sort of idea seems to hover in the minds of both Tawney and Kraus. It is true that they speak of 'later' Puritanism, the 'true and genuine' Puritanism, as a powerful agent of economic progress. But this 'later' Puritanism was created by the impact of emergent capitalism upon the 'earlier' Puritanism to which capitalistic modes of thought were alien. Robertson, however, develops the theory of the converse correlation with consistency and aplomb. As was mentioned earlier, his argument can be summarised in two propositions: (1) the fact that the capitalism of the new age revealed itself first in Protestant countries is due to the geographical discoveries. The latter shifted the economic centres of the world westwards away from Italy; (2) the fact that the most capitalistic nations were Protestant, particularly in the mercantile and similar classes, is due to the greater ease with which new ideas spread to trading nations and persons.

It cannot be denied that the discoveries were obviously of tremendous significance. In his eagerness to turn Weber's correlation upside-down, however, Robertson seems to be guilty of dangerous simplifications and exaggerations. Firstly, lively economic interrelationships were enjoyed, even before the great geographical discoveries, by many of the countries that turned to one or another form of Protestantism. Secondly, in many instances it was manifestly not economic relationships but connections of another kind that were decisive in giving currency to the doctrines of the Reformation. So far as Lutheranism is concerned, its dissemination in Germany was, so to speak, a given product of the geographical location of the reformer himself and the eagerness of certain principalities to win their independence from the Holy Roman Emperor as well as the Pope. Most of those who carried the new doctrines to Scandinavia were not businessmen but students, returning home from German seats of learning where they had become disciples of Luther. Later on, conversion did not come about as a result of particular classes—and still less the great masses—of society being influenced by other nations, but through government decree. The same is true of the Reformation in England. It was the breach with the Papacy and the destruction of the feudal power of the church that were the main issues, not the propagation of novel doctrines among either the mass of society or certain sectors of it.[1]

The situation in the Reformed church countries was different. But Robertson's interpretation does not completely fit into this picture either. Geographically, Switzerland's conversion is self-evident: it was there that the whole business started. The advance down the Rhine to certain regions of France and the Netherlands followed traditional economic and cultural routes that had been used for hundreds of years. Calvinism won its chief successes in France in regions and in circles where the pressure of strong reformatory currents had been felt even be-

---

[1] For economic relations before the great discoveries, see J. Kulischer, *Allgemeine Wirtschaftsgeschichte des Mittelalters und der Neuzeit. I. — Das Mittelalter* (1928); H. Pirenne, *Economic and Social History of Medieval Europe* (1936); G. Espinas, *Les Origines du Capitalisme* (2 vols., 1933—36); H. Sée, *Les Origines du Capitalisme moderne* (1926). See further, Latourette, *op. cit.*, p. 766, who stresses that 'in France the Protestant Reformation came from several sources,' with roots in humanism and with its dissemination in court circles, as well as through students and business men. Many of the most active Huguenots, moreover, were officers and noblemen, not business men. In many walks of life, furthermore, 'national loyalty and religious fervour were combining' (*ibid.*, p. 770). How difficult it is to determine the limits of such concepts as 'rising middle class' or 'declining aristocracy' is abundantly clear from the dispute between R. H. Tawney and H. R. Trevor-Roper on whether the English gentry, around 1600, were rising or falling in the economic and social scale. See R. H. Tawney, 'The Rise of the Gentry, 1558—1640,' *Economic History Review*, Vol. XI (1941), pp. 1—38 and H. R. Trevor-Roper, *The Gentry, 1540—1640* (*Supplement to the Economic History Review*, 1953).

fore Calvin. To bring the geographical discoveries and *new* trade routes into this picture is pure nonsense. Moreover, there was a political background to the appeal of the doctrines in the Netherlands. The ideal of independence that they contained accorded well with the struggle for liberation from the Spanish-Habsburg yoke. It might well be supposed that the strong link between Spain and the Catholic church made the latter unpopular at the same time as the Spanish hegemony was becoming abhorrent. On this point, however, it is essential to remember that for a great many people it was in a context of indifference rather than of religious ardour that conversion to Calvinism took place; and, moreover, that Calvinism in its more austere form never achieved major influence in the Netherlands. In the leading circles of that country it was religious toleration rather than Reformist fanaticism that predominated.

It is more difficult to distinguish any generalised trends in the growth of the free church sects, for on the whole their scope tended to remain rather localised. The rallying of the Scots to Presbyterianism surely needs to be viewed against the background of, *inter alia,* Scotland's general political and cultural pattern, and in particular the clan system and the distrust of England. Of course, business connections may to some extent have provided a channel for the dissemination of such creeds as Methodism, Quakerism and Pietism. In England, for instance, as some scholars have pointed out, the firm hold of the Established church on the landed nobility, resulting from such factors as patronage, may have helped to make the nonconformist sects attractive to business, artisan and industrial circles which were often hostile to the landed interest; to small traders on their way up socially and economically; and to elements of the landed nobility in social and economic decline. But the direct missionary zeal of religious fanatics also enters into the picture. The adoption of free church doctrines in certain regions of Europe, for instance, can be largely 'explained' by reference to the heavy emigration from those regions to the United States.

It was from the United States that many of the preachers came who were responsible for the work of conversion. These American missionaries concentrated their main effort upon the European countries and provinces of origin of the sects that financed them. It was, in general, through a variety of ways and means and interrelationships that the different creeds were carried to new countries and classes of people. To try to distinguish a single principal avenue of dissemination is a fruitless undertaking. Trade may have had something to do with it, perhaps a great deal—thus far Robertson is right. But to make this the prime and almost only important explanation is to force the argument beyond the bounds of the permissible.

It is clear that the geographical discoveries definitely shifted the centre of gravity of trade and industry to western Europe. But this is also a vastly simplified statement. The discoveries, or at all events the establishment of trading factories and colonial empires, were, to put it very roughly, not only a 'cause' of the rise of western Europe, but also an 'effect' of that rise, of the force of economic and political expansion. The economic centre of gravity had long been moving north-westwards. The cutting-off of Italy from important trading regions by the Mohammedans, the rise of the Hanseatic League, and the emergence of England and the Netherlands from at least the 13th century onwards, had sapped and begun to demolish the Italian supremacy. In this connection it ought to be noted too that the cultural vigour of Italy as the fountain head of Renaissance learning *may* have caused the economic importance of that country to be over-estimated. It may be that, measured in terms of volume of trade, industrial production and general economic buoyancy, the Netherlands and Hanseatic territories were not so very far behind Italy and the Italian merchant cities from the 13th century onwards. Be that as it may, however, it seems beyond dispute that behind the discoveries and the ensuing colonisation there lay a political and economic expansiveness that had long been building up among the nations principally active in these enterprises. The inference is that the discoveries cannot possibly constitute the primary explanation of the subsequent vigour of the Protestant countries.

As mentioned earlier, it was Cunningham, before he succumbed to the influence of Weber and Troeltsch, who was the foremost advocate of the second possibility—that economic progress and the spread of Protestantism may each have 'derived' from wholly extraneous factors. Cunningham explained the rise of 'modern' capitalism in terms of the disruption of the social system of Catholicism in the 15th and 16th centuries under the impact of new national states, new kingdoms and principalities, hostile to the papal power. This generated competitiveness and dynamism; the factors that made for inertia in the old social order were vanquished. The interesting feature of this theory is that secularisation, not religion, is postulated as the vital factor.

Thus far it seems as though Cunningham was right in holding that economic expansion and hostility to the temporal power of Pope and church exhibited a degree of 'co-variation,' advancing hand in hand through the 14th, 15th and early 16th centuries. The practical application of Reformation ideas—in many states by royal ordinance—was the last phase of the break with Rome. However, this does not necessarily imply that the rise of modern capitalism became possible *because* the social system of Catholicism was demolished; if we are to deal in terms of Cunningham's conceptions at all, it would seem more likely that in many countries the status of Catholicism in society was undermined by the emergence of capitalism— quite independently of how and why capitalism was spreading. To assert that the appearance of national states hostile to the papal power created the prerequisites of economic expansion seems a little far-fetched. If this sort of correlation is to be argued at all, would it not be more plausible to declare that incipient, or in some places fully developed, economic expansion towards the end of the Middle Ages established one of the most vital preconditions for opposition to the authority of Rome? It was an England with a long history of economic development behind it that severed the connection with Rome; in Sweden it was a sovereign power that had been mustering its financial and political might over a couple of hundred years; in Germany it was the stronger princes who nerved themselves to cast the die. It was after Luther felt the need of princely support that the theory of the prince as temporal head of the church was added to Lutheranism.

However, before trying to explain *why* Protestantism and economic progress were associated, some attempt should be made to determine *whether* in fact there was any association at all of the sort taken for granted by Weber, Cunningham, Tawney, Robertson and other authors referred to in the opening chapter of this book. In other words, does the problem, upon the solution of which so much intellectual effort has been expended, really exist?

It is impossible to answer this question in terms as general as those which have been used so far. A study of the problem in the most important states, one by one, is needed. Was the Weber correlation a fact in the development of the most important post-Reformation economies? To the extent that it was a fact, was the nature of the co-variation such that a causal relationship operating in one direction or the other can reasonably be postulated?

2. PROTESTANTISM AND PROGRESS

Broadly speaking, there is some truth in the contention that the Protestant countries, and especially those adhering to the Reformed church, were particularly vigorous economically. Thus far we can agree with Weber. But the correlation is far from complete. None of the regions mentioned is characterised by such symmetry in terms of religious faith and economic progress as is necessary if correlations of this type are to be meaningful. So many important reservations have to be made that the hypothesis as a whole becomes untenable. Virtually everywhere in the Protestant regions, persons of deviant religious persuasions were successful entrepreneurs. A reference to the Jews may suffice. The same conceptions as were propounded by Weber in regard to adherents of the Reformed church have been argued by others, principally Sombart, in relation to the Jews. In some places, Catholics and Lutherans—alleged by Weber not to be particularly able—have played an important part in economic life in the midst of groups where the Reformed faith predominated. It is in Belgium perhaps that the Catholic contribution has been most notable. But England was not untouched by it; nor, certainly, were the Netherlands in the 16th and 17th centuries. Moreover, it is far from true that all the 'Protestant' regions displayed especial economic vigour. Nor would it be correct to assert that the 'Catholic' regions were on the whole 'economically under-developed'.

By the time Luther and Calvin were born, the Low Countries and the northern and western districts of Germany had already been characterised for at least three to four hundred years by exceptionally brisk economic activity: textile manufacturing and commerce in the Netherlands and Flanders; ironfounding, salt-drying and international trade in the Hanseatic territories. And in England, too, economic life had begun to exhibit great liveliness well before Henry VIII demanded the annulment of his first marriage.

The economic golden age, the beginning of which in the Netherlands is usually assigned to the 16th century, had its roots in an expansive trend that began several centuries before the foundation of the Reformed Church.[2] By the close of the 13th century, at least, the Netherlands had won a position in the front rank of textile manufacturing and trade. Furthermore,

[2] See above p. 93 n. 10; Baasch, *op. cit.*, esp. p. 6 ff. The idea that the 'spirit of capitalism' of the Dutch derived from their Calvinistic dogma is, writes Baasch, 'schwerlich richtig'. Cf. Beins, *op. cit.* See further I. W. van Ravesteyn, *Onderzoekningen over de economische en sociale ontwikkeling van Amsterdam gedurende de 16de en het eerste kwartaal der 17de eeuw* (1906), pp. 272—362; Hyma, *op. cit.*, pp. 321—43; P. Geyl, *Debates with Historians* (1955).

103

the Netherlands reaped an advantage from the decline of other mercantile regions, especially the Hanse towns of Germany.[3] This decline became most marked after the Reformation had conquered a number of the most important of those towns. If their decline were to be interpreted in accordance with Weber's method, then the inference would be that economically the Reformation affected them in an adverse sense. This was plainly not so. The decline had commenced earlier; and it gained momentum with the re-orientation of the pattern of trade into routes more advantageous to the Netherlands and England, and with the liberation of the Scandinavian states from their earlier economic and political dependence upon the German merchant cities.

In his work on the economic history of the Netherlands, Baasch gives sufficient factual evidence to justify the definite rejection of the idea that the 'spirit of capitalism' in that prosperous country was created by Calvinism.[4] It was not until well into the 17th century that Calvinism prevailed in Amsterdam, the most important mercantile city, and this change was of an entirely political nature, being occasioned by adherence to Maurice of Orange. The great Dutch merchants and industrialists made but one important demand in religious matters: that the complete freedom to which they were accustomed in trade and enterprise should be paralleled in the sphere of religious life by similar freedom to choose their doctrine and belief. It was the prerogative of the individual to decide which religious faith he should follow. Toleration—and in many quarters indifference—became the characteristic feature, and was expressed for instance in the opening of the frontiers to Jews and other groups persecuted on the ground of religious faith. Many of the largest merchants in Amsterdam were Catholics, and celebration of the Catholic Mass had long been far from un-

[3] On the Hanse see esp. E. Daenell, *Die Blütezeit der deutschen Hanse* (1905—6); F. Rörig, *Hansische Beiträge zur deutschen Wirtschaftsgeschichte* (1928); K. Kumlien, *Sverige och hanseaterna* (1953).

[4] See esp., p. 7 f.

usual. More than two-thirds of the population of the Netherlands professed Catholicism by the end of the War of Liberation—in the more important cities the preponderance was even greater. In his study of economic and social conditions in Amsterdam in the 16th and early 17th centuries, van Ravesteyn reaches the conclusion that it was among the better-off sections of the community that Catholicism maintained its grip the longest. To quote one of his examples: Jacob Poppen was the mayor of the city at the beginning of the 1620s and probably its richest inhabitant. His wife and son were Catholics. Van Ravesteyn further emphasises that it was among the poorest classes that Calvinism first spread. The most fanatical Calvinists were drawn almost without exception from the lower strata of society. The large merchants and industrial entrepreneurs were generally indifferent.[5] 'There is no doubt,' writes Hyma, 'that the poorer classes of people in Amsterdam and elsewhere looked up to the church as the necessary means of salvation, whereas the more prominent men and women saw much that was good in all religious denominations, and, as a result, were not so easily awed by the authority of Calvinist clergy'.[6]

Both Baasch and Hyma stress that Amsterdam was moving towards its leading position during the Middle Ages. During the 16th century this process continued apace. Judging by the Öresund customs accounts, Holland enjoyed a clear predominance in the important Baltic navigation and trade as early as 1503—at a time when no Protestants and scarcely any Jews were to be found in the Netherlands at all. Of 1,222 vessels registered through the Sound in that year, 718 were stated to be from Holland.[7] Hyma also points out that the province of Friesland shows a steady rise, sustained over a long period, in its parti-

---

[5] van Ravesteyn, *op. cit.*, p. 272 f.
[6] Hyma, *op. cit.*, p. 340.
[7] See N. E. Bang & K. Korst, *Tabeller over skibsfart og varetransport gennem Øresund 1497—1660* (1906).

cipation in Baltic navigation; after the province becomes Protestant a clear decline is apparent.

In his collection of essays, *Debates with Historians,* one of the most distinguished Dutch historians, Geyl, examines the theory that the Netherlands succeeded in liberating themselves from Spain because they were Protestant while Belgium failed in its fight for freedom because it was Catholic. Geyl demonstrates how mistaken this theory is.

It implies, he writes, 'that it must have been because Protestantism steeled the Northern rebels—the Dutch—to a successful resistance, while the Southern rebels—the Belgians—being Catholics did not have the heart to preserve in the struggle. It is the answer which is still to be found in innumerable English and American textbooks and which indeed until fairly recently used to be given, in various disguises, or to a greater or lesser extent attenuated or qualified, by both Dutch and Belgian historians. But it never agreed with facts.'[8]

When the insurrection began, the Protestants were no more numerous in the north than in the south. It was not the climate of opinion but strictly geographical and strategical considerations that prevented the rebels from pushing southwards and the Spaniards from pushing northwards. The line that separated them followed the selfsame river system that held up Field-Marshal Montgomery at Arnhem for eight months in 1944: 'The true explanation, then, of the division of the Netherlands into a Protestant North and a Catholic South is the exact opposite of the current one. It is not because the South was Catholic and the North Protestant that the rebellion failed here and succeeded there: it is because the rivers enabled the rebellion to entrench itself in the North provinces while Spain recovered those situated on the wrong side of the strategic barrier that in course of time there sprang into existence this dual system of the Protestant Northern Republic and the Catholic Southern Netherlands, of Protestant Holland and Catholic Belgium.'[9]

[8] Geyl, *op. cit.,* p. 182.
[9] *Ibid.,* p. 184.

There may be some justification for believing that the combination of Spanish tyranny and the general 'freedom' of commerce and business, characteristic of Dutch cities long before the Reformation, prepared a particularly fertile soil in the Netherlands for Calvinism and its demands for religious freedom. In any event, it is obvious that Dutch economic success was achieved without the aid of any strong state power or of an inter-city organisation of the Hanseatic type, and that, in the field of direct business enterprise, firms were on the whole more simply organised and individually managed than was generally true elsewhere. An early developed economic individualism, an early initiated struggle for what may be termed the right to political individualism: these were followed only rather later, in the course of the 16th and 17th centuries, by a transition to the form of relative religious individualism represented by the Calvinist reformation as compared with the earlier Catholic state church.

Such is the sequence of events. In other words, the economic rise of the Netherlands cannot be explained in terms of religious changes. To credit that rise to the account of religious beliefs is no more justifiable than it would be to ascribe the relative decline of the Netherlands in the late 18th century to a similar cause.

Parallel considerations apply to England. In all branches of English economic life the seeds of a perceptible expansion were germinating from at least the beginning of the 13th century. The network of foreign trade was widening and important technical innovations were taking place, especially in the textile industries. 'All through the centuries since 1100 there had been progress, slow and intermittent but real, in various branches of industrial technique,' sums up Clapham.[10] The boom started so

[10] J. Clapham, *A Concise Economic History of Britain from the Earliest Times to 1750* (1949), p. 225, see in general pp. 125—72. See also G. N. Clark, *The Wealth of England from 1496 to 1760* (1946); J. Clapham, *Commerce and Industry in the Middle Ages* (1929); L. F. Salzman, *Eng-*

long before the Reformation and reached full maturity so long *after* it that it is fruitless to try to interpret the course of events in terms of a religio-economic correlation. To do so could only result in a hopelessly confused assessment of the degrees of effect produced by the Reformed state church, the Puritans, the Methodists, the Quakers and Scottish Presbyterianism.

It is true that the first Empire was built up after the great geographical discoveries (for which the Catholic nations were responsible in the first place) and for the most part after England had gone over to Protestantism. But this occurred as the accompaniment of a bitter struggle for power with Spain, a struggle that never accomplished its aim of breaking the Spanish hegemony in South America; and the expansion of English power certainly did not happen as suddenly as its assignment to the Elizabethan age would imply. At the accession of Elizabeth it was still impossible for anyone to foresee that England would be able seriously to dispute the control of the sea with France, and still less with Spain.[11] In fact, however, the prevailing political situation was swiftly transformed beyond recognition, 'was becoming rapidly an anachronism'. The English held certain assets the value of which was still not understood by their neighbours:

'Disruptive feudalism had destroyed itself in the baronial faction wars and had been replaced by a strong national monarchy. A rising industrial and commercial class began to take advantage of the fact that the main stream of European trade was flowing past its doors. At the same time it reinforced the political structure by blending itself with the territorial aristocracy. Furthermore, the Islanders had a natural aptitude for the sea, matured in the hard school of the Iceland fisheries and in stormy voyages to Bordeaux and Oporto. When they had acquired the techni-

lish *Industries in the Middle Ages* (1923) and *English Trade in the Middle Ages* (1931); E. Power, *The Wool Trade in English Medieval History* (1941).

[11] V. T. Harlow, *The Founding of the Second British Empire* (1952), p. 12 ff.

que of ocean navigation from the pilots of Spain and Portugal and made themselves pioneers in ship construction and had also become the inventors of a new system of naval tactics, they were qualified to grasp the decisive weapon of sea power.'[12]

The assignment of historical dates to broad trends of a social and economic nature is always hazardous. Everything turns upon the question of which among the many influences at work is to be given the greatest weight. The tendency to foreshorten perspectives, to increase dramatic tension by ignoring the fact that the underlying condition of any particular historical situation often took a long time, perhaps hundreds of years, to develop fully, is very common both in historical works and in popular opinion. That Rome was not built in a day we may remember, but we forget, for example, that behind Gustav Vasa's organisation of the Swedish national state there lay the work of financial, economic and political concentration and reconstruction that was carried out in the preceding century. In face of the definitive fall of Antwerp, the two hundred-year climb of Holland and Amsterdam is overlooked. We tend to ignore the fact that English and Dutch expansion in the 17th century was preceded by a long period of gathering strength; and that at about the same time France experienced a violent expansion—as did Spain and Portugal nearly a hundred years earlier—in which great riches were amassed, new trade routes opened, new shipbuilding techniques devised, and a new art of navigation discovered. When English sea-power began to take shape under Elizabeth, the Puritan movements had still not secured any hold upon major sectors of the English community. It was from high church and in some cases Catholic circles that the great sea-rovers and empire-builders chiefly stemmed.

In Scotland, which Weber and Cunningham held to provide such an important proof of the economic effect of religious doctrines, economic expansion did not begin to make itself felt until well into the 18th century. It is probably impossible to deter-

[12] *Ibid.*, p. 12.

mine what the causes were. However, perhaps one of the principal factors to be taken into account in any explanation is the substantial trade with the American colonies that the union with England enabled Scotland to build up on the basis of the Navigation Acts. The centre of this trade, in which the most important commodity was tobacco, was Glasgow. It was an entrepôt traffic: the tobacco was re-sold to France, England and other European countries. The War of American Independence, which cut these links, also threatened for a time to shatter the structure of Scottish commerce. The situation was saved by an increase of trade with the Netherlands and the West Indies and the development of maritime carrying for other nations. The trade with the West Indies was particularly effective in stimulating the growth of a Scottish cotton industry. From the Scottish point of view, the spinning machines of Arkwright and Crompton certainly appeared at an opportune moment and, by the same token, so too did the new bleaching process, discovered in France. M. L. Robertson suggests that the War of American Independence thus forced the Scots into the textile industry, after Scottish enterprise had been animated and Scottish capital resources built up by the American trade.[13]

Whatever the detailed facts of the situation, this much is clear: that the expansion occurred after the Calvinist-Puritan spirit had lost its power, after secularisation and the Enlightenment had become more important influences than religious zeal. This does not necessarily imply that it was secularisation and the Enlightenment, the tempering of the Puritan spirit, that generated progress. But it does mean that under no circumstances can we look to the specially rigorous Scottish form of the Calvinist Creed, Presbyterianism, in seeking its cause.

To turn to Switzerland.[14] Was it with the Reformation that

[13] M. L. Robertson, 'Scottish Commerse and the American War of Independence,' *Economic History Review,* Vol. IX (1956); see also on Scotland, Bryson, *op. cit.,* pp. 5—7, 25—28; and H. Hamilton, *The Industrial Revolution in Scotland* (1932).

[14] See W. Martin, *Histoire de la Suisse* (1926); E. Gagliardi, *Geschichte der Schweiz* (1938); J. I. Good, *History of the Swiss Reformed Church*

Switzerland became prosperous? Is it to Calvinism that we must point as the economic mainspring of the Confederation? The hypothesis is not easy to support; on the contrary, it falls apart even on the most superficial scrutiny of the country's history. Other factors weigh much more heavily in the scales: principally the region's favourable position as a focus of trade and communications between Italy and northern and western Europe, and the difficulty its inhabitants had in winning an adequate livelihood from agriculture. Long before the Reformation, indeed long before the introduction of Christianity, Switzerland was a country with a highly developed commercial life; Caesar was able to enumerate no less than twelve established market towns in what were then the provinces of Gallien and Rhaetia. The whole history of the Confederation ever since the cantons of Uri, Schwytz and Nidwalden formed the Everlasting league in 1291 seems to have been associated with emancipation from traditional feudal ties through the rise of important cities whose liberties derived from trade, industry and economic stability. In Switzerland the saying 'Die Stadtluft macht frei' took on a meaning far deeper than for most of the German free cities.

Did Switzerland enjoy a further and more intense economic boom during the Reformation or so soon after it that a positive cause-and-effect relationship can plausibly be inferred?

Nothing of the sort seems to have been seriously asserted by any scholar. It is not until the 18th century that a clear move in such a direction is observable. That century brought a large-scale expansion of Swiss industries that had long been active. This development manifested itself in such varied phenomena as the growth of watch and clock manufacturing in the west and of cotton manufacturing in the east. A sharp increase of population and the limited productiveness of agriculture in the cantons gave the Swiss solid reasons for experimenting with forms of activity aimed at export markets. It does not seem judicious to correlate this process of industrialisation with reli-

since the Reformation (1913); S. Kraft, *Schweiziska Edsförbundets tillkomst* (Historiska studier till Sven Tunberg, 1942).

111

gious attitudes. The German-speaking districts for the most part profess the Zwinglian variety of Reformist doctrine, which according to Weber takes a more tepid view of business life, usury, diligence and thrift than Calvinism, the main strength of which is in the French-speaking provinces. But it would not be true to assert that the latter were economically more advanced than the former after the beginning of the 16th century. As for Geneva itself, Calvin's principal base and the centre from which his teachings were propagated, before Calvin, even before the Reformation, it had been an important centre of trade and industry; and an economically powerful citizenry had succeeded, as early as 1287, in extracting a substantial measure of independence from their ecclesiastical overlords.

Not even the contention that is basic to Max Weber's thesis—the correlation between Protestantism and economic progress in Germany—seems to hold water. Here too there are factors other than religious conditions that can more plausibly explain the situation in the various regions of the country: the deposits of iron and coal in the west, the trade routes along the Rhine, the extent and profitability of agriculture in the east and south. Moreover, the Protestant element in the major industrial and commercial districts is far from preponderant. In Essen about half the population is Catholic, in Dusseldorf a good two-thirds, in Cologne—the largest city of western Germany— at least three-quarters. Indeed, during the period of industrialisation the Catholic predominance in all these places was even more evident. Furthermore, it may be noted that many of the most prominent industrialists, businessmen and bankers were Catholics and/or descendants of families whose wealth and noble rank dated back for generations, whose mode of life and general outlook assort extremely ill with Weber's theories.[15]

[15] On Germany see in particular, P. Koch, *Der Einfluss des Calvinismus und der Mennonitentums auf die Niederrheinische Textilindustrie* (1928) and J. Hashagen, 'Kalvinismus und Kapitalismus am Rhein,' *Schmollers Jahrbuch,* Vol. XLVII (1924), pp. 49—72.

Another region whose progress has been very largely attributed to religious attitudes is New England which, as the native heath of Benjamin Franklin, is of special interest in this context. Why, people have asked, did the industrialisation of the United States, particularly in the field of textiles, begin in New England? Why not in the South, the land of cotton? The accident, if indeed it was an accident, that a certain Mr. Samuel Slater, who disembarked in New York in 1789 with the jealously guarded English manufacturing secrets in his baggage, betook himself to Providence and Pawtucket rather than to Atlanta, Charleston or New Orleans, cannot constitute the whole explanation, even though mere accidents often seem to have exercised a very great influence on economic happenings, and especially on what is usually termed the location of industry. Insofar as certain natural prerequisites were needed, such as good transport facilities, water-power and a humid atmosphere, the South could offer these just as much as the North. And similarly in other branches—metals and minerals, leather and fish: in all of them, there are no disparities of access to raw materials, power or transport facilities sufficient to explain why the industrialising process of the late 18th and early 19th centuries started in New England rather than in the South.[16]

So the field has been clear for Weberesque notions. Book after book and essay after essay have hammered at the theme of the austere Puritan spirit and its inculcation of diligence, thrift and the will to succeed. That Benjamin Franklin happened to be born in Boston was indeed to be accounted a happy event for proponents of this theme.

It cannot be denied that, in New England, diligence and thrift and the urge to attain a good economic position were ideas which enjoyed a superior social *éclat* than in most other regions.

[16] Apart from general writings on American economic history such as H. U. Faulkener, *American Economic History* (1943), W. W. Jennings, *op. cit.*, and C. A. Beard, *Making of American Civilization* (1937), see on New England in particular J. T. Adams and others, *New England's Prospect, 1933* (1933); C. A. Beard, *Economic Origins of Jeffersonian Democracy* (1943); and A. Schlesinger, Jnr., *The Age of Jackson* (1948).

But it would be prudent to enquire whether these characteristics may not have emanated from quite other factors than the purely religious one. Moreover, important parts of the South originally had Puritan leanings. Puritanism cannot properly be postulated as an explanation without first elucidating why it was that its hold was particularly strong in the six states of the north-east. The South still lags behind the North economically; but Puritanism has long been more prominent in the South than in the northern states, where secularisation soon occurred. It is impossible to apply to New England the theories that may appear plausible elsewhere—theories that religious nonconformity produced an indirect effect because dissenters formed an isolated group, cut off from society as a whole, excluded from the public service and therefore more amenable to the attractions of trade and industry than ordinary people; or that the special quality of their education was particularly effective in developing the capacity to devise technological innovations.

The great difference between New England and the South lay in the extent and fertility of arable land. In the South: vast and productive tobacco and cotton fields. In the North: small farms nearly everywhere, usually yielding very poor returns. In one, extensive cultivation characterised by plantations, slave labour and mild winds not unfavourable to growth; in the other, single-family agriculture characterised by small units and an adverse climate. In New England one had to go outside agriculture to attain wealth, or indeed even a slightly above-average livelihood. The fur trade, fishing, maritime carrying and the slave trade soon became the most important branches of economic life. And these were occupations in which, because they yielded larger profits than could be had from other trades, a surplus of capital was created that could be made available for new and more ambitious projects. If this theory is sound, than a particularly marked propensity to accumulate capital and take risks must have been prevalent in New England—because these qualities were necessary there for success and well-being.

114

Add to this another important factor, which may of itself provide a satisfactory partial explanation of the association between religious zeal and economic success apparent at first sight in New England. The first really big wave of immigrants came from England in the 1630s, during the reign of Charles I. The causes are not easy to determine; starting with Tawney's 'Rise of the Gentry', a whole literature on the social conditions of this period has developed. But as has been pointed out in a fairly recent work,[17] two points about this migration are clear: (1) the migrants were Puritans; their faith was certainly the principal conscious cause of their migration, even if there were difficulties of English economic life that contributed. (2) But faith alone did not carry people across the Atlantic and enable them to sustain themselves in the New World while they broke the ground or established their business. The poor had no alternative but to stay at home. Those who went on their way were relatively well-to-do, often of the artisan and tradesman class. New England received thousands—including woman and children it may have been as many as 20,000 persons—of comparatively well-off persons skilled in trade and handicrafts. This surely goes a long way towards an explanation. That these people were also Puritans and were impelled to leave largely because of their Puritan faith is another matter, and quite unconnected with Weber's correlation argument.

Just as it is possible to 'explain' the economic vigour of New England without having recourse to religious concepts, so presumably can other instances be similarly explained. Wherever Weber saw Protestants and the Reformed church, other factors can be found that are far more obviously calculated to promote trade and industry, capital formation and economic progress. England, the Netherlands, Scotland, the North Sea and Baltic districts of Germany, Switzerland—they all furnish examples: their location on ocean shores of transcontinental routes that

[17] A. French, *Charles I and the Puritan Upheaval. A Study of the Causes of the Great Migration* (1955).

were in use hundred of years before the Reformation; the definitive shift of the centre of gravity of European trade to the North Sea and Atlantic as a result of the great discoveries and the throttling of the Mediterranean routes by the Arab countries; the frequent inability of agriculture and stock-raising alone to provide adequate sustenance.

Amongst the lowland regions of eastern and central Europe, whether Greek Orthodox or Roman Catholic, Lutheran, Zwinglian, Calvinist or Sectarian, there is nothing to choose: nowhere were trade and industry on a major scale in evidence. Had Italy and Spain been converted to the Calvinist creed in the 16th century or later been flooded with Puritans and Pietists, trade would still not have remained centred on the Mediterranean but would have shifted to the coasts of Holland, England and Germany.

Take Portugal, for instance. In that country the late 13th century saw the commencement of a boom in mining and trade, the latter being largely based on the cultivation of the vine. This trend continued into the 14th and 15th centuries. Portugal became a commercial, seafaring and exploring nation, with names such as Henry the Navigator, Diaz, Vasco da Gama and Cabral to add lustre to its annals. For a time Lisbon was the centre of world trade. The Portuguese state owned one of the world's foremost trading companies. Then military defeat, a demographic foundation inadequate to support the swiftly-acquired colonial empire, and lastly the Spanish invasion, brought the edifice down in ruins. But in the midst of these ruins Lisbon continued to function as one of the principal entrepôt ports of the European colonial trade.[18]

But, to 'explain' this expansion—which carried Portugal at one bound to a position of importance, perhaps for a time supremacy, in world trade, relegating the Italian merchant cities to the background—in terms of religious changes, is impossible.

[18] H. Heaton, *Economic History of Europe* (1948); E. Prestage, *The Portuguese Pioneers* (1934); and C. R. Beazley, *Prince Henry the Navigator* (1904).

We can point to the reorientation of trade routes that was in progress even before the Reformation, to successful voyages of discovery, to a succession of powerful regents, and perhaps to the toleration that until the 16th century was extended to the Jews, who had to depend largely upon trade for their livelihood and who often enjoyed special advantages conferred by their international family relationships. But we cannot speak of any 'capitalistic spirit' engendered by religious faith.

The industrialisation of England and Belgium is particularly interesting. To explain why these countries were the first to industrialise is an undertaking upon which we shall not embark. There are certainly many factors worthy of notice. But we cannot measure their internal significance. We cannot even determine whether the absence of one or another of them would have retarded or precluded industrialisation.[19]

To make a comparison with a country which became a powerful industrial nation much later, England differed from Germany at the end of the 18th and beginning of the 19th century primarily in its national unity, which had been maintained unbroken for centuries. In England there was a fairly integrated market within a comparatively small area with well developed communications. Add to this the empire, which formed an additional source of raw materials and a partial outlet for finished products, and the contrast of markets with Germany, split as it was into a host of principalities, becomes very striking. Furthermore, England experienced relatively early the emergence of a fairly broad 'middle class,' i.e. of groups with purchasing power adequate to support industrial 'mass production'.

England differed from France and other mercantilist countries

[19] Apart from sources already cited, see J. Clapham, *Economic History of Modern Britain* (3 vols., 1926—29); J. L. and B. Hammond, *The Rise of Modern Industry* (1926); F. A. Hayek (Ed.), *Capitalism and the Historians* (1954); J. H. van Houtte, *Esquisse d'une histoire économique de la Belgique* (1943); F. Baudhuin, *La structure économique de la Belgique* (1926).

by virtue of the gradual disintegration of the system of economic regulation and corporate enterprise during the internal dissensions of the 17th and 18th centuries. Central authority never lost its grip on the body politic for very long. The market was not dismembered. But the mercantilist apparatus of control, sustained and exploited by gilds, corporations or chartered companies, broke down. Although still very much alive on paper, it signified little or nothing in practice. This apparatus of control had been contrived largely in order to protect the old-established economic organisations in trade, handicrafts and manufacturing from the competition of new types of enterprise. We know what difficulty new manufacturers must once have had to force an entry into the traditional, monopolistic system, and how difficult it must invariably have been for new forms of enterprise to prevail against the old wherever the latter were bolstered by organisations enjoying the support of the state. It is therefore easy to understand how greatly the decay of *dirigisme* and the system of monopolies facilitated the industrialization of England. Furthermore, a social revolution was working in the same direction. On the one hand there was the comparatively early rise of a fairly broad 'middle class', in the sense defined above, and on the other, the early disruption of older social forms through the growth of population, the transformation of agricultural operations by the enclosure movement, and the emergence of a large landless class from which the new industrial districts could quickly recruit their supplies of labour.

The unity of the market and the wider freedom of movement for new enterprise were supplemented by an abundance of capital, low interest rates and a raw material, coal, that was vital to the new technology. If to this is added the fact that some of the most important inventions happened to be either made in or carried to England, then a large number of the most vital prerequisites of the industrial revolution in that country have been listed.

But was no influence exerted on all this by religion, by the strong Puritan element present in English society—and in particular precisely amongst those groups who, according to many observers, were chiefly responsible in their primary capacity as inventors and entrepreneurs for the industrialization of England? Perhaps an answer to this question can be supplied by a comparison with trends in Belgium. Belgium, of course, was the next country to industrialise and it therefore affords a particularly interesting contrast. A number of factors may be considered that seem to merit inclusion in any explanation of the rapid industrialisation of Belgium.

Belgium had long been one of the foremost centres of manufacturing, especially of textiles. The Napoleonic Wars and the Continental System had forced industrial growth, as in a hothouse. The old system of regulation and the former ascendancy of gilds and companies had perished. Access to ore and coal; copious influx of capital which had long been flowing from Dutch mercantile houses; a geographical location propitious for the development of communications: to these important elements in stimulating Belgian industrialization must be added the pool of occupational skills, which had been a feature of the iron industry in the Walloon areas of the country for generations and which the new industrial districts could now exploit.

With the best will in the world, this country, for hundreds of years in the vanguard of economic advance and now pressing close upon the heels of England in the race to industrialize, cannot be fitted into the Weber framework. Belgium is and always has been quite overwhelmingly Catholic. (For a long time it had been anti-Jesuit Catholic too, and so does not fit the Robertson hypothesis either). Only two or three per cent of the inhabitants belong to non-Catholic denominations. Of these, something like half have been Jews in the last few centuries. The most important business and industrial districts have always been Catholic. The Protestant element, formerly as now, is so insignificant as not to be worth mentioning in the present context.

Thus, for both England and Belgium we can trace a number of factors, similar in kind, that may be seen as vital preconditions of the early arrival of the industrial revolution in these two countries. In the light of this knowledge, there is nothing puzzling in the fact that Belgium very quickly followed along the trail blazed by England—except from one angle of approach: if we start from the assumption that Weber was right. The great contrast between England and Belgium lay in the domain of religion. According to Weber's theory, Belgium ought to have lacked the most vital prerequisite of an industrialization that was very nearly as rapid as that of Protestant, Puritan-influenced England. But this difference brought no corresponding difference in economic expansion.

Of course, the association in Belgium of Catholicism and vigorous economic growth does not in itself exclude the possibility that Protestantism in general and the Puritan sects in particular made a substantial contribution to the economic development of England. But Belgium does at least supply a strong indication that Protestantism and Puritanism were not ingredients wholly indispensable to an economically progressive environment. At all events, food for thought is provided by the reflection that the one factor alleged by Weber to form a common characteristic of the successful should also be the principal factor differentiating the two most successful.

It seems, then, that even before the Reformation strong tendencies towards economic expansion were making themselves felt in the Netherlands and England; and that no correlation or 'co-variation' between economic and religious trends in these countries can be established. In Scotland and Switzerland, the sequence of events differs. Here, despite the fact that both countries were Protestant from the 16th century onwards, economic expansion does not begin until well into the 18th century, and it is then evident that its impetus derives from quite other factors than the religious. In New England too, despite a correlation that certainly appears superficially strong, we have been unable to find anything suggesting the existence of a connection, in the deeper meaning of the word, between Puritanism and capitalism; the Puritan South—for it has long been much more Puritan than the states of the North—is economically 'under-developed'. Portugal, an entirely Catholic country, was long in the van of the great expansion of the 15th and 16th centuries, and its chief mercantile city is still an important maritime and commercial centre. Catholic Belgium was the first country in the world to industrialize after England; and it retains its status in the comity of industrial nations despite the ravages of two world wars.

Having established these points, we can move on to the second of Weber's correlations: the association between religious faith and business aptitude in certain of the Free Protestant groups.

3. THE FREE CHURCHES AND ECONOMIC PROSPERITY

That there was a connection between religious views and economic status even within the individual denominations of the various countries, and that, in the midst of other Protestants, the Puritans and Free Church sects generally were possessed of special economic aptitude, are propositions that in Weber's eyes constituted a qualification of the hypothesis that Protestant countries achieved special success.

This hypothesis has been generally accepted. Quakers, Huguenots, Methodists and so on have been attributed with special economic ability, universally valid, by scholars in many fields. On this point too, however, the explanations have varied. Though Weber, like Cunningham and Tawney, saw a direct connection between Puritanism and the economic activities of these groups, other authors have suggested other explanations. It has been said that it was the sense of rejection and estrangement from society, combined with actual isolation from influence and power, that induced or simply compelled nonconformists to 'get on by themselves'; no other road to social and economic advancement than their own enterprise was open to those barred from the service of the state and the established seats of learning. As a variation on this theme, it has been suggested that religious persecution, by stimulating emigration from certain countries and immigration into others, promoted the dissemination of occupational skills and internationalism.

Such explanations are categorically rejected by Weber. To admit their validity would deal a mortal blow to his whole theory of a direct relationship between religion and economic progress. It would suffice for the purpose of the present criticism of Weber if we could concur in these alternative hypotheses. However, this cannot be done without substantial reservations. Even if Quakers, Methodists, Huguenots and so on did sometimes display a particular aptitude for economic affairs, closer inquiry reveals, as in the discussion of the Protestant countries as a whole, that the entire conception of correlation and co-variation is, to say the least, doubtful.

In his *Iron and Steel in the Industrial Revolution*, Ashton pauses to note the great contribution of the Quakers to the English iron industry: 'In the early years of the eighteenth century perhaps the most numerous, and certainly the most successful and progressive group of iron masters was that made up of Quakers: indeed the more important chapters in the early history of the iron industry might be written almost without passing beyond the bounds of the Society of Friends. At one time or other Quakers were to be found conducting iron works in each of the chief centres of production.'[20]

Later on, however, Ashton's narrative discloses that nearly all the important entrepreneurs of Quaker faith in the iron industry were relatives of, or had married into, the great iron-founding family of Darby. All the persons concerned are Darby's sons, cousins, sons- and brothers-in-law, and in one of two cases his employees: William Rawlinson, Richard Ford, Richard Reynolds, Thomas Harvey, Anthony Parker, the Cranage brothers, John Hawkins, Charles Lloyd, the Pemberton family, John Fidoe. They made up a clan of Quakers and ironfounders, about which it is impossible to generalise how far marriage led to business connections and involvement in the

[20] p. 213.

iron trade and how far business connections led to marriage. The fact that Quakers only married Quakers—they were forbidden to go outside the circle—strengthened the bonds of the clan.

But this feature is certainly no unique phenomenon requiring interpretation in terms of mystical economic driving forces generated by religion. On the contrary, in all occupational groups the union of business and family relationships was a normal feature of this period everywhere in the Western world.[21] Masons married mason's daughters; merchants' sons married merchants' daughters. It was not unusual for a clever young bookkeeper or other 'superior' employee of a firm to be translated to the status of partner and son-in-law at one stroke. In view of the importance attached to religious considerations in that age, it is not surprising that religion should have played a significant part in bringing about marriages between people of the same sect.

Consequently, when for one reason or another, two or three Quaker families became prominent ironfounders, it is not in the least extraordinary or unexpected if a number of Quakers eventually made their mark in the same branch of industry. If the Darbys had been Methodists or Huguenots, there is no doubt that Ashton could have written in precisely the same terms—and Weber would have found it an excellent illustration of his theme—with the sole different that the word Methodist or Huguenot would have been substituted for Quaker. If the Darby family had been Jewish and, through intermarriage, brought a number of other Jewish families into the English iron industry, then we could have expected Werner Sombart to point gleefully to this striking example of the role of the Jews. During the great waves of immigration into England in the 19th century, Jews tended perceptibly to gravitate into certain specialised branches of business life. As has been shown by Lipman,[22] there are numerous factors that may account for this, such as their oc-

---

[21] For some examples, see Samuelsson, *op. cit.*

[22] V. D. Lipman, *Social History of the Jews in England, 1850—1950* (1954), *passim.*

cupations in their respective countries of origin, conditions in the regions where they settled, language difficulties, the law of the Sabbath, the influence of relatives already established—all explanations analogous to the 'family theory' developed above. But what if the Darbys had been Catholics and a number of Catholic families had achieved eminence in the iron industry? In that event, Weber and his disciples would no doubt have dismissed the whole affair as an exception, no more worthy of mention than the similar case of Belgium. To point again to an example already adduced, there was no place for the Brentano family.

As was mentioned earlier,[23] Ashton refers again in one of his later works to the influence of nonconformists during the industrial revolution.[24] He quotes a number of the inventors and business pioneers of the industrial revolution who belonged to such dissenting denominations as the Quakers, Methodists, Baptists, Unitarians, Congregationalists, and Scottish Presbyterians. As a variant upon Sombart's theory of 'foreigners' and 'heretics' or 'outcasts', Ashton develops what may be termed the 'education theory'. The exclusion of nonconformists from schools and universities had induced the various Free Church sects to establish numerous seats of learning of their own. By contrast with the ordinary schools, these educational institutions concentrated largely upon research and instruction in technical subjects and the natural sciences. This gave to dissenters—the argument is limited to Great Britain—a specially marked capacity to participate in the work of technological and entrepreneurial innovation characterising the age of the industrial revolution. Dissenters were 'rejected' by society and therefore had to take their education into their own hands; they accordingly directed their education towards those spheres of life open to 'outcasts'; this resulted in the development of a special aptitude for invention and enterprise.

There is no doubt that the observations on which Ashton

23 Above, p. 22.
24 *The Industrial Revolution,* p. 17 ff.

bases his theory are correct. His portrayal of the Free Church educational system is a true one, and his references to its bias accord with the facts. But it must be stressed that the bias towards practical subjects and the natural sciences exhibited in these schools and universities was to a very large extent an accompaniment of the increasing popularity of Enlightenment philosophy, of secularisation and the demand for freedom from religious dogma in research and education; and thus it was not primarily related, if at all, to the quest of 'outcasts' for their own special fields of activity.[25]

There are, however, other and weightier objections to Ashton's theory. Firstly, his observations apply only to Great Britain: no comparable features have been described in other regions where the Free Church sects are supposed to have been of similar economic significance; whatever else may be said about the Puritans of New England, they were certainly not 'outcasts' in the land of their adoption. Secondly, it has never been proved, and can surely never be proved, that the contribution of the nonconformists to England's industrial transformation was really as important as Ashton and many others before him have asserted. Even if any major proportion of the inventors and business pioneers of late 18th and early 19th century England belonged to nonconformist rather than other denominations; even if there was a certain 'over-representation' of dissenters —and this cannot be established—nevertheless nearly all sectors of the population, or at all events of the upper and middle classes, *were* represented. Nor must it be forgotten that roughly half the inhabitants of England belonged to nonconformist denominations at the time of the industrial revolution. If approximately every other prominent businessman or inventor was a nonconformist, this tells us nothing about the influence of religious beliefs or Free Church schools upon enterprise—and no one has yet been able to show that such a proportion was reached, and still less that it was substantially exceeded.

[25] On the English school system at the time, see McLachlan, *op. cit.*

Considered as a whole, it is clear that exaggerated notions have grown up about the importance of a single phenomenon, quite simply because this particular phenomenon happens to have been especially discussed and noticed. Weber and others referred to the role of the Reformed religion in general and the Free sects in particular; and so every nonconformist entrepreneur and inventor is marked down with special zeal. In Holland, Weber attracted no attention until the 1930s; then suddenly the impact of Calvinism upon the economic life of that country began to be emphasised, despite the fact that no one had ever previously hit upon the idea of a connection between the two features. (Nor has anyone subsequently succeeded in proving such a connection.)

This over-valuation is surely similar to that placed upon the role of the Huguenots and the Jews. Sombart naturally regards the expulsion of the Huguenots from France in 1685 as a very important event, and in this he is undoubtedly right. A body of people characterised by skill in business and enterprise enriched the economic life of other lands, perhaps Prussia most of all: thus is the phenomenon usually depicted.

It is true that the Huguenots were very largely merchants and businessmen.[26] But this was not necessarily because their religion impelled them into enterprise. It could just as easily be—if any connection is to be assumed at all—that in France, as in certain other places, the Reformed doctrine was especially attractive in certain petty bourgeois circles because of its general demand for freedom. It is clear that on the whole the Reformed Church's adherents among the business classes were at issue not only with the religion prescribed by the state but also with the economic policy largely dictated by 'high finance' in Paris. But in all probability it was not simply a matter of merchants who

26 J. Vienot, *Histoire de la Réforme Française* (2 vols., 1924—26); W. E. J. Berg, *De réfugiés in de Nederlanden na de hercoeping van het Edict van Nantes* (1845); L. van Nierop, 'Stukken betr. de nijverheid der réfugiés te Amsterdam,' *Econ. Hist. Jaarbock,* VII and IX (1921 and 1923).

thus stood in opposition becoming Huguenots. It is probable that to some extent Huguenots espoused a business career so as to achieve that measure of independence which undoubtedly was often a prerequisite of 'daring' to be a Huguenot; and conversely, free merchants, economically independent of the state as they were, found it easier than most to deviate from the general religious persuasion. We must think in terms not of *one* explanation but of a series of individual explanations.

When the Edict of Nantes was revoked, only the most ardent and tenacious remained loyal to their faith even at the cost of persecution and exile. The great majority yielded before the threat of expulsion or death and went over to Catholicism. In these circumstances it is not strange that Prussia and other countries enjoyed an influx of able persons commanding a range of occupational skills and a degree of entrepreneurial initiative that would not otherwise have been offered to them, or at any rate not at such a moderate price. The businessmen who went into exile were an *élite* consisting of the toughest, most tenacious and self-reliant, and certainly more well-to-do of their kind, who, possessing money and business connections abroad, found it comparatively easy to make a niche for themselves in their countries of adoption. Though it should be added that in the Netherlands, at least, the great mass of the Huguenots seem to have become soldiers and officers.

How much the Huguenot immigration signified in the wider perspective it is obviously impossible to say. Even the fact that it was to Protestant and Reformed church countries that the Huguenots took themselves needs to be carefully scrutinised. If the Protestant religion was peculiarly efficacious in developing human aptitudes, then of course this ought to have applied to the natives just as much as to the Calvinists expelled from France. To measure the effects of their assimilation by the different countries will not be an easy task if religion is regarded as the determinant of ability.

There has undoubtedly been a strong tendency to over-estimate the influence, in purely quantitative terms, of the

Huguenots, just as there has been with the Jews and other 'foreigners'. Foreign names always claim more attention than indigenous names. A hundred Prussians and ten Huguenots tended to mean 'many Huguenots,' simply because the latter attracted special notice. Every time people came across a French-sounding name in a business context, the comment: 'Another of these Huguenots' came readily to the lips. It is the same sort of fallacious reasoning, magnifying 'some' into 'many', from which the Jews have so often suffered. The presence of a few Jewish businessmen and financiers in the top levels of business life has been sufficient in the eyes of many for 'high finance' as a whole to be regarded as 'run by the Jews,' despite the fact that the Jewish element in the top levels of the world of high finance, both American and western European, has been fairly inconsiderable. The role of the Jews in Amsterdam during that city's era of supremacy was always considered quite decisive in its significance. That the Spanish régime drove the Portuguese Jews into exile was its great economic blunder; that the Dutch admitted them was Holland's good fortune. And of course the addition to the stock of business skill and connections represented by these Jews was of great importance. But, as is stressed by Bloom in his penetrating study of the subject,[27] it has all been wildly exaggerated. The Jewish element was not as important numerically as had been believed, and its qualitative role was far smaller than was generally supposed. The drama of their exile from Portugal and migration to Netherlands, together with their survival as a minority isolated by religion and race, inflated their numbers and importance in the popular and scholastic imagination. Only a few of the really large mercantile and banking houses of Amsterdam's golden age were of Jewish lineage.

Similar considerations apply to Sombart's theory of 'foreigners' and 'outcasts'. It was not religious concepts but religious per-

· [27] H. I. Bloom, *The Economic Activities of the Jews of Amsterdam in the Seventeenth and Eighteenth Centuries* (1937).

secution in some quarters and toleration in others that decided
the issue. These were the instruments, says Sombart, by which
occupational skills were disseminated and groups formed in the
society to which business came readily because of their international connection. But in the long view, 'alienship' arising
from religious persecutions was only a part, and not a large
part, of an important general trend: an interchange or 'internationalisation,' so to speak, of merchants and other categories
of entrepreneurs.[28]

An important feature in practically every land and age has
been the operation of external impulses transmitted by immigrants and continuing for generations by virtue of the bonds
linking immigrants and their progeny to the 'old country'. In
Sweden, for example, a harvest of occupational skills was reaped
by its ironfounding industry from the Walloons in the 17th
century, by its manufacturing industry from the Germans and
Dutch in the 17th and 18th centuries, by its export trade from
the English, Germans, and Norwegians in the 19th century.
In the 17th, 18th and 19th centuries, immigrants from Scotland
and England, from Holland and France, from Germany and
the Baltic states, also forged important trade links between
Sweden and the great commercial centres of Europe. Similarly,
in the Netherlands, it is not difficult to point to a number of
great immigrant financiers and merchants, mainly from England and Scotland, but also from France, Switzerland and Portugal. The Jews exiled from Portugal may be particularly mentioned in this context. All over Europe, both during and after

[28] For the following account of 'foreigners' and 'internationalisation',
see Samuelsson, *op. cit.*, and the works quoted therein; esp. E. Sandberg,
'Merkantilism och kyrkopolitik,' *Kyrkohistorisk årsbok,* 1949; H. Levin,
*Religionstvång och religionsfrihet i Sverige 1686—1782. Bidrag till den
svenska religionslagstiftningens historia* (1896); J. Mathorez, *Les étrangers
en France sous l'Ancien Régime* (2 vols., 1919—21); H. Sée, 'Le commerce des étrangers, et notamment des Hollandais, à Nantes,' *Tijdschrift
voor Geschiedenis* (1926); Wilson, *op. cit.*; J. E. Elias, *De Vroedschap
van Amsterdam 1578—1795* (2 vols., 1903—05); E. Arup, *Studier i
engelsk og tysk Handels Historie. En Undersøgelse af Kommissionshande-
lens Praksis og Theori i engelsk og tysk Handelsliv 1350—1830* (1907).

the pre-industrial era, deliberate efforts were made on the one hand to attract foreigners to one's own shores, and on the other hand to set up one's own business houses abroad. These tendencies were perhaps most apparent in the 18th century. Although merchants were assimilated quickly enough in their adopted countries, they developed a kind of international freemasonry of business, with relatives and intimate connections in all the large commercial centres of Europe.

These efforts both to create an international trade network and to increase the supply of occupational skills by immigration often lent importance to the admission of people expelled from other countries by religious persecution. The Netherlands and the Portuguese Jews provide a good example. The demand for religious freedom was early linked to conceptions of the beneficial effects of immigration.

In Sweden, as early as the 17th century, Johan Clason Risingh, then the foremost Swedish writer on economic subjects, attached considerable weight to freedom of worship. He regarded it as an essential prerequisite for attracting merchants and capitalists into the country. Risingh lays particular stress on the experience of Holland. It is freedom of worship that made Holland 'rich in people and money'.[29] At the beginning of the 18th century Johan Silfvercrantz, eager for the creation of a Swedish manufacturing industry, put forward the same argument; in a letter to Charles XII during the latter's sojourn at Bender in 1710–11, he advocated liberty of worship for the reformed churches. The first real economic writer in Sweden, Anders Nordencrantz (1699–1772), also underlines the importance of religious freedom, and on the same grounds. Nordencrantz, however, treats it as one aspect of the wider demand for freedom in all forms. The need for religious freedom is a continuous theme in the reports of the Swedish Board of Trade (*Kommerskollegium*) in the early 18th century. After prolonged debate, toleration was extended to the Reformed church by a decree of 1741; the so-called Edict of Toleration (*toleransediktet*)

[29] See E. Sandberg, *op. cit.*

followed in 1781 and Gustaf III's Edict on the Jews (*Jude-edikt*) in 1782, both of these being similarly dictated by the need to attract able businessmen into the country. The large proportion of businessmen among Jews in Sweden was at first quite simply due to the fact that only Jews engaged in trade were admitted—and the influence of these early immigrants upon those who came later persisted for some time; immigrant Jews who were master tradesmen or intended going into business were more likely to have relatives or friends in Sweden willing to help them.

However, by no means all 'foreigners' were affected by religious persecution or toleration. Most of the British merchants in Sweden in the 18th century went as agents of their family firms to watch over their interests in Swedish exports—or had gone there because they knew, from experience of Swedish exports of iron to England, that there was money to be made in Sweden. The same is true of English merchants in the Netherlands—two of whom, Hope and Clifford, founded financial and mercantile houses which were at times the largest in the Netherlands—and to Dutch merchants in England. International contacts, the need for an intimate knowledge of market conditions in a variety of places despite difficulties of communication, the desire of young sons of merchants to see the world and learn the languages and customs of other countries—there are plenty of reasons to account for the establishment of a profusion of foreign houses all over Europe. Religious persecution was only one of these reasons, even though a very important one.

Some examples, mainly from the 18th century, may serve further to illustrate these observations.

There was a marked tendency for merchants to develop trade with those nations with which their own governments had particularly active connections. In Bordeaux at the beginning of the 18th century, there were special courses in Dutch to facilitate intercourse between natives and Dutch merchants. Of the 509 merchants, bankers and manufacturers who, on the 2nd March 1789, were trading on the Bordeaux stock exchange,

Dutchmen and Germans accounted for 95. La Rochelle and Nantes also had many Dutch merchants at this time. Names such as Haerzel, de Wich, van Woorm, van Heulen, Maetzuyer and Haentjens were still to be encountered in Nantes in the early 1920s; all were descendants of the Dutch merchants of the 18th century. The main reason for these Dutch settlements in France seems to have been the passive character of French trade; in the 18th century Dutch merchants controlled much of France's export trade.

Merchant houses of Dutch origin were not uncommon in England. Examples include John and Wolfert van Hemert, London correspondents of de Neufville's and Peter Grellius, Gilbert de Flines and Willem Kops, London correspondents of David Leeuw's. Several countries of western and northern Europe had merchant houses in the Mediterranean region: in 1670 in Leghorn, for example, there were reported to be no less than 24 such English houses.

The situation in Amsterdam, however, is particularly interesting. Of the really prominent merchant houses, only that of Pels, was of Dutch origin. The first known member of the family, Andries Pels, was born in the Netherlands of Dutch parents in 1591. Cliffords were descended from an English immigrant merchant of the late 17th century, George Clifford, who founded the firm. By about 1712 his son George was already numbered amont the financial magnates of Amsterdam; in that year he negotiated a loan to the ruling house of Austria. The founder of the firm of Hope was a Scottish merchant who settled in Rotterdam in 1664. The Hopes' period of greatness began in the mid-18th century. From the 1770s onwards it was long regarded as the foremost banking house in the world. After the crisis of 1773, it concentrated entirely upon financial operations. The firm of Hogguers commenced with the arrival of Jacques Cristoffel Hogguer from France in the 1720s. The family claimed that, originating in Sweden, it had emigrated to St. Gallen in Switzerland during the early 17th century and then moved in the next generation to France

132

—Lyons at first and Paris later. There, the four brothers Mark Fredrik, Daniel, Laurent and Jean Jacques established the banking firm of Hogguers Frères. Jacques Christoffel was Daniel's son. The Grill family was of a similar international stamp. From Italy, where they were called di Grillo, the Grills had found their way, via Augsburg and the Netherlands, to Sweden, where Anton Grill achieved among other things the office of *riksguardien*. One branch of the family remained in Sweden while another returned to Amsterdam. Descendants of the Amsterdam branch came back to Sweden again as early as the second generation. The Hasselgrens were of Swedish lineage, while the Petersens came from Denmark (the town of Rendsburg, in Holstein), whence Jakob de Petersen emigrated to Utrecht at the end of the 17th century. The de Neufville family, of which the great Dutch merchant Jan Isaac de Neufville was a member, owed its origin to the arrival in the Netherlands of Jean de Neufville from Frankfurt.

The Hogguers provide an illuminating example of the predilection of these 'foreigners' for doing business with their countries of origin. Jacques Christoffel, who started his firm in Amsterdam in 1722, built principally on the foundation of his connections with Hogguers Frères in Paris. His son Daniel, who in 1762 went into partnership in Amsterdam with Jan Jakob Horneca to form the firm of Horneca, Hogguer & Co., seems to have maintained these French connections. The links with Sweden were important too, both in the lifetime of this partnership and in those of its successors—Horneca, Fiseaux & Co. (1773–79), Fiseaux, Grand & Co. (1779–87) and then Hogguer, Grand & Co. After 1770 a considerable number of Swedish government loans were negotiated through the firm. Financial connections were also maintained with Switzerland.

A feature of the foreign merchant houses—or merchant houses of foreign origin—in 18th century Sweden that is of more general interest should be noticed. In the 1760s the foreign names of British and French origin largely disappear from the front

133

rank of commerce in Stockholm and are succeeded by German and to some extent Dutch names. The phenomenon as a whole is none too easy to explain. The disappearance of many of the old names does not in itself pose any insoluble problem: the crisis of 1763, together with the normal departures, by death or retirement, of business leaders provides sufficient explanation. The generation that came to the fore after the Great Northern War was going into retirement by the 1760s. Other firms besides those of British or French origin were overtaken by a similar fate at this time or a little later.

But what does need explaining is the fact that British immigration ceased while the German continued as before.

The resumption of peaceful conditions in Scotland after the rebellions of 1715–16 and 1745–46 may have affected the volume of British immigration. It was mainly Scots who emigrated to Sweden. And the union of the crowns of England and Scotland facilitated, at least in time of peace, Scottish emigration to England. There was, however, another and probably more important, factor. The British interest in Sweden was primarily concerned with Swedish iron. The merchants of British origin were all prominent in the export of iron, chiefly to England. It is true that interest in Swedish iron did not vanish completely in the middle years of the 18th century. But, like the interest in Scandinavia and Baltic generally, it lost ground in relative terms, as Britain's advance towards a position of economic world power started gathering momentum. One consequence of this was that British merchants, or impecunious noblemen, could now find more important and lucrative forms of employment for their sons than appointments as commercial representatives in Stockholm and Gothenburg.

The same observation can be made in regard to English emigration to the Netherlands. The truly important Dutch merchant houses of British origin had been established in the late 17th and early 18th centuries. Later on in the 18th century, no British immigrant managed to attain any notable place in the ranks of such houses. Since this can scarcely be attributed to any absolute decline of interest in the Netherlands, it may be inferred that expansion elsewhere in the world was chiefly responsible. The need to have merchant houses of one's own was presumably regarded as more pressing, and the chances of rapid success more favourable, in regions where new interests were being planted than in those already well cultivated.

There was no simultaneous relative diminution of north German interests in Sweden. These interests were bound up with Swedish exports and still more with Swedish imports, principally of grain. Sweden's balance of trade with the Baltic states was heavily in deficit. Grain, of which the latter area was the almost exclusive source from the 1760s onwards, generally constituted the largest proportion by value of imports into Stockholm during the period 1730–1820. Substantial quantities of textiles, another important category of imports, only slightly below grain by value, also came from this region.

It seems reasonable to infer a connection between Sweden's switch from the Baltic states to north Germany as a source of imports and the influx of north German merchants and their families into Stockholm. Since many of these merchants soon became large exporters as well, the switch produced an impact on the export trade as well. While British immigrants came to Sweden principally as buyers, Germans came as sellers. The leading importing firms were almost exclusively of German origin throughout the 18th century.

It is plain that in all these instances it was commercial interests that dictated immigration, not *vice versa*. The capacity of business houses with a German background to hold their own against rival houses of other origins was increased by the sensitivity of the grain trade to cyclical fluctuations. This rendered necessary a specially intimate relationship between exporters and importers. Obviously, some of the firms in question had come to Stockholm partly to act as agents of exporting interests in their home countries. By degrees all of them entered other fields of enterprise too, developing an import business in other commodities and with other areas as well as engaging in the export trade, though continuing to concentrate mainly upon the Baltic states.

These examples, which could be multiplied, seem to show clearly that for the most part the 'role of foreigners' was quite unassociated with religious persecutions. Certainly the Anglican and Presbyterian Englishmen and Scots who founded merchant houses in the Catholic Mediterranean region were not motivated by them, any more than were the large Dutch colonies in French ports. Nor did they affect the streams of German immigrants into Sweden or the Swedes who settled in other countries —England, the Netherlands, Portugal, Spain and Italy—and there established businesses trading principally with firms in their countries of origin. How large a part religious exiles played in the whole picture of events it is impossible to say. But, it was certainly not their activities that set the fashion. On the contrary, they went where others had gone before. Forces far more powerful and universal than religious persecution motivated what may be called the 'internationalisation of business'. To the extent that religious considerations did affect the issue, the connection was for the most part merely passive, in the form of permission being granted to foreigners of alien faith to work in the various countries concerned: Reformed church adherents in Lutheran states; Anglicans, Reformed church members, and Lutherans in numerous Catholic regions. In many places it was a couple of hundred years after the Reformation before the idea of toleration began to gain general acceptance. Consequently, the Reformation, with its splintering of religious faith and its destruction of the sense of solidarity that Catholicism had given to the whole Western world, surely also produced a delaying effect upon the 'internationalisation of business'. To try to determine which was the more important in the long run, this impediment upon international mobility or the stimulus to mobility represented by religious persecution, is a profitless undertaking.

This is an appropriate point at which to re-examine the observation, fundamental to Weber's thesis, that in regions of Germany where religious faiths were mixed, Protestant children were sent more usually than Catholic children to schools where the mode of instruction was particularly suitable for future merchants and industrialists; and that Protestant journeymen were more ready than Catholic to abandon handicraft work and become artisans rather than masters. In this Weber saw one of the mystic effects of religious belief.

The first thing to be said about the influence upon journeymen of membership of a particular religious faith is that, insofar as any generally significant and statistically verifiable variation in the volume of movement into industry can be revealed, factors quite other than *die geistige eigenart*[30] could clearly have been responsible; for instance, the industrial demand for artisans may have chanced to be particularly brisk or the opportunities for making a living out of handicraft work particularly few in some of the Protestant districts. But aside from the fact that a variety of explanations is possible, to construe the movement into industrial wage-labour as a sign of the economically progressive spirit of the individual is surely a most curious hypothesis. Save for a few particularly unremunerative handicraft trades outside industry and a few well-placed groups of artisans within it, it was more desirable to become a master tradesman than a factory worker. The economic, social, and perhaps also the cultural, standard of the former was, or was believed to be, far superior to that of the latter. And it is still much the same today; that it was so in Weber's time and during the *Gründerperiod* that was nearest to him is beyond question. The skilled factory workers of that era were nowhere particularly numerous, particularly well educated or particularly well paid.

Furthermore, quite apart from considerations of social and

[30] See above, p. 3.

economic status, the master tradesman as a rule certainly carried a heavier economic responsibility than the wage-earning artisan and had a great need of the 'spirit of enterprise'. The master tradesman was not infrequently the very man who developed into the industrial entrepreneur. And in that case, Weber's own information shows that the Catholics, not the Protestants, should be regarded as being the better endowed with the 'spirit of capitalism'.

Weber clearly attached much more importance, however, to the data extracted from Offenbacher's paper, classifying pupils at non-obligatory secondary schools by religious faith.[31] Weber reproduces one of Offenbacher's tables, showing that in 1895, while 37 % of the inhabitants of Baden were Protestants, 61 % Catholics and between 1 and 2 % Jews, 48 % of secondary school pupils were Protestants, 42 % Catholics and 10 % Jews.[32] Both Offenbacher and Weber were at pains to stress the extreme importance of the fact that this relative Protestant preponderance was particularly noticeable in the *Realgymnasien* and *Oberrealschulen*. (We may for the moment ignore the fact that a typographical or arithmetical error—see p. 140 below—led them to overvalue the proportion of Protestants by ten units, equivalent to a good 15 %.)

Weber offers no figures other than those above. But Offenbacher also gives figures for the population of Baden as a whole, classified by religious faith: Protestants 638,000, Catholics 1,057,000, Jews 26,000, making a total of rather more than 1.7 millions. Neither author tells us how many pupils there were in the schools investigated. However, the *Statistiches Jahrbuch für das Grossherzogthum Baden* for 1895–96 discloses that the total numbers for that academic year amounted to 14,587 pupils, of whom 12,138 were male. All the girls attended special *Mittelschulen für die weibliche Jugend* and are of no interest in the present context. The table which follows classifies the 12,138 boys by religious faith and types of school:

---

[31] Offenbacher, *op. cit.* See above, p. 2.
[32] *Protestant Ethic,* p. 189.

	Protestants	Catholics	Jews	Others	Totals
Gymnasien	2,073	2,095	329	26	4,523
Realgymnasien	787	577	137	3	1,504
Oberrealschulen	789	648	89	12	1,538
Realschulen	1,537	1,317	337	16	3,207
Höhere Bürgerschulen	655	551	160	0	1,366
Totals	5,841	5,188	1,052	57	12,138

In his table of percentages, Offenbacher used average figures for the years 1885–95. The percentages he obtained therefore differ from those which can be derived from the table for the academic year 1895–96. The comparison is very interesting:

	1895—96			
	Protestant	Catholic	Jews	Total
Gymnasien	46	47	7	100
Realgymnasien	52	39	9	100
Oberrealschulen	52	43	5	100
Realschulen	48	41	11	100
Höhere Bürgerschulen	47	40	13	100
Totals	48	43	9	100

	1885—95			
	Protestant	Catholic	Jews	Total
Gymnasien	43	46	9.5	98.5
Realgymnasien	59	31	9	99
Oberrealschulen	52	41	7	100
Realschulen	49	40	11	100
Höhere Bürgerschulen	51	37	12	100
Totals	48	43	12	100

The aggregate average for the academic year 1895–96 corresponds fairly closely with that derived from an average calcula-

139

tion for the decade 1885–95. But the disparities as between the various categories of school taken separately are notably less marked in the academic year 1895–96. Protestants are about as numerous as Catholics in the *Gymnasien;* in the *Realgymnasien* and *Oberrealschulen* their preponderanc~ is much less considerable; and in the *Realschulen* too the proportions are rather more even. (Through a typographical or arithmetical error, Offenbacher also made the proportion of Protestants in the *Realgymnasien* 69 % *instead* of 59 %; Weber later took over and used this incorrect figure.)[33]

It would certainly be wrong to view these differences as indicating a trend; such deviations arise from fluctuations in particular years. If we refer back to 1884, the year before Offenbacher's averages start, the proportions are more similar to those of 1895 than to the averages for the intervening period: the Catholic aggregate is 43 %, with 47 % in the *Gymnasien,* 36 % in the *Realgymnasien,* 42 % in the *Realschulen* and 40 % in the *Oberrealschulen.*

At this stage it is imperative to evaluate these figures and their fluctuations; a matter which Offenbacher and Weber evade by giving only relative figures. Of the 12,000 persons concerned in 1895—and the proportions were similar in 1884—4,500, which is to say nearly 40 %, went to the *Gymnasien,* the division between Protestants and Catholics being generally about even. Only 1,500 went to *Realgymnasien,* i.e. only 12 % of the total. No reliable evidence can emerge from a comparison between the percentage proportions of Catholics and Protestants comprised in the whole population of 1.7 millions and the corresponding proportions in a total of 1,500 school-children. For only relatively small absolute movements of the latter figures are needed to change the percentage figures appreciably, as the discrepancies between Offenbacher's average values and the values for 1895 also demonstrate. One newly-established school in a district with a preponderance of Catholic or Protestant inhabitants is sufficient to distort the statistics.

[33] See the table in *Protestant Ethic,* p. 189.

This brings us to a particularly serious point. Neither Offenbacher nor Weber tried to ascertain in what proportions the various denominations were represented among the inhabitants of those school districts where Protestants predominated in the schools. Let us take the *Realgymnasium,* in which, according to Offenbacher, 59 % of the pupils were Protestant and according to the figures for the academic year 1895–96, 52 %. These schools turn out to have been situated in the following districts: Karlsruhe, Mannheim, Ettenheim, Mosbach, Billingen and Weinheim. If we count only the two Christian denominations, in 1895 almost exactly 55 % of the inhabitants of these districts were Protestants. Even in detail, the conformity is so close that in Ettenheim and Billingen, where Protestants accounted for only 13 % and 32 % respectively of the Christian population, they accounted for 13 % and 23 % respectively of the Christians in the *Realgymnasien.* In Buchen, Schweitzingen, Wiesloch and Ettlingen there was a group of *Höhere Bürgerschulen,* separately recorded in the statistics, to which Catholics contributed 59 % of the Christian children. In these districts Catholics constituted 58 % of the population. In Schweitzingen Protestants were rather more numerous both in the category of school in question and in the population as a whole. In the city of Baden there were twice as many Catholics as Protestants; the Catholic enrolment in the Baden *Realschulen* was almost exactly twice the Protestant. In Ueberlingen and Waldshut, with over 70 % Catholics, the *Realschulen* were over 70 % Catholic.

Thus, school by school and district by district it appears that the proportions of school children classified by religious faith are almost exactly the same as the corresponding proportion of the total populations of the appropriate district. That the Protestants in Baden as a whole display a 'school frequency' higher than their share in the aggregate population is thus due entirely to the fact that more Protestants than Catholics lived in districts where *Realgymnasien, Höhere Bürgerschulen* and *Realschulen* were available. If one reckons not in terms of total population but of inhabitants of districts containing the respective categories of schools, there remain no differences worth mentioning.

How trivial the business was, even on Offenbacher's own accounting principles, is disclosed by certain data that he regards as specially significant. In the years 1891–94, he declares, 35 Protestants but only 14 Catholics chose the career of an officer. In what way the officer corps could be considered more 'capitalistic' than the priesthood, which was a more usual career amongst Catholics, is not specified. 11 Protestants and 9 Catholics went in for accountancy, 142 Protestants and 111 Catholics chose the law, and 54 Protestants and 51 Catholics entered medicine. In civil and mechanical engineering and chemistry there were 54 Protestants as against 22 Catholics. At the same time, however, Catholics preponderated in the two economic fields of public finance and financial legislation—in both cases 71 % of the total. Veterinary surgeons were almost wholly Catholics; the larger landed estates in Baden were almost all owned by Catholic families.

To draw conclusions about *die geistige Eigenart* of Protestants and Catholics respectively, from such figures as these is surely absurd. The whole Weberian correlation, based on school conditions in Baden, turns out to hinge upon the simple fact that in certain towns with a particularly large Protestant majority in a country otherwise predominantly Catholic there were more Protestants than Catholics at the secondary schools. If the religious denominations of the children are compared with demographic conditions in each individual school district, Catholics and Protestants exhibit precisely the same 'propensity for schooling'. In brief, Weber's alleged difference is a myth.

In addition to the schools, first Offenbacher and then Weber refer to the distribution of wealth.[34] Protestants are said to be richer than Catholics. It is evident that the material produced as evidence is, to say the least, unreliable, consisting as it does of taxation figures. Methodologically worse than this, however,

[34] Offenbacher, *op. cit.,* Weber, *Protestant Ethic,* pp. 35, 188.

is the fact that the material is dragooned into yielding conclusions that would be inadmissible even if the sources were unexceptionable.

In 1897, taxable wealth in Baden amounted to 4.7 milliard marks. Of this 1.6 milliard belonged to Protestants, 0.3 milliard to Jews and 2.8 milliard to Catholics. Thus Catholics held about 60 % of the total wealth known to the tax inspectorate; in other words, their share of statistically recorded wealth corresponded almost exactly with their representation in the total population. But, says Offenbacher, the situation is different where interest on capital is concerned. There it is the Jews who come first, followed by the Protestants. Here is his table, using the original nomenclature of the Grand Duchy of Baden, so as to avoid all confusion of meaning:

Capital attributable to: (percentages)	Protestants	Jews	Catholics
1. Grund-, Häuser- und Gewerbesteuer	28.1	4.4	67.5
2. Spezielle Einkommensteuer	37.2	7.5	55.3
3. Kapitalrentensteuer	45.5	8.3	46.2

Offenbacher is only interested in item 3, where Protestants were 'over-represented'. At the 1895 census, he adds, the capital assets comprised in this item worked out at 4.1 million marks per 1,000 Jews, 0.95 million marks per 1,000 Protestants and only 0.59 million marks per 1,000 Catholics. This, he claims, reveals the intimate connection between the superior education of Protestants and their higher incomes.

In fact, on Offenbacher's own mode of calculation it is the Jews whose average wealth in terms of this form of capital asset stands revealed as noteworthy. The difference between Protestants and Catholics is moderate by comparison. So, *die geistige Eigenart* must have been particularly well developed among the Jews, whom we have already seen to have been 'over-represented' in the schools. The true explanation is quite different and more credible. In Baden there happened to be a relatively large number of rich Jews and not very many poor ones, and since it was only exceptionally that landed property entered into the composition of Jewish fortunes, the fortunes of rich Jews were channelled into forms of investment that weighed particularly heavily under the heading *Kapitalrentensteuer*. A study of Russia, Poland or the United States, for example, where there were large numbers of poor Jews at this time, would have produced low average values. Thus, the same Judaism that promoted business aptitude in certain states engendered business ineptitude in others. Very odd.

Yet the situation of the Protestants is in principle the same. As we have seen from the foregoing, they tended to live in towns to a far greater extent than the Catholics; obviously this would cause them to invest their money differently. Offenbacher has this situation clearly in mind when discussing real assets; he cites figures which disclose that 61.5 % of the Catholics but only 46.5 % of the Protestants lived in communities with less than 2,000 inhabitants, while 24.3 % of the Protestants but only 13 % of the Catholics lived in communities with over 20,000 inhabitants. A comparison of urban with rural Catholics revals the same differences in the form of capital investment as Offenbacher postulates for Protestants as compared with Catholics. Regional distribution, not religion, is the primary factor.

This raises a further question. May there not have been religious causes leading to this Protestant preponderance in towns, especially the larger ones? Does not a correlation exist after all, even though Offenbacher and Weber discovered it by the roundabout route of 'school frequency' and distribution of wealth instead of by exploring residential distribution direct? The possibility obviously cannot be dismissed out of hand. But in the first place, it is clear that the whole line of reasoning becomes much more complex than it would be if it could be shown that, *under otherwise similar circumstances,* Protestants displayed a greater 'propensity for schooling' than Catholics.

144

It is *a priori* arguable that *die geistige Eigenart* might affect this propensity, the form taken by capital accumulation, and similar direct patterns of conduct. That it should also promote human migration on any appreciable scale is a notion that carries little plausibility—it should be observed that this is not a question of migration occasioned by religious persecution but by *die geistige Eigenart,* in other words, it was voluntary, or as one might say, generated solely by 'inner compulsion'. In the second place, quite a large measure of correlation could exist between Protestantism and residence in large towns without the explanation necessarily being that people were impelled by their religious faith to congregate in towns. Protestantism was the new religion. It is not inconceivable that in certain parts of Germany the towns were the easiest places for disseminating propaganda; more people were reached, perhaps less conservative resistance was encountered than in the country—and, moreover, the ideology of the French Revolution made its strongest appeal to urban dwellers. It is not impossible that townspeople may have become Protestants because they were townspeople, thus luring Offenbacher and Weber into making false correlations from such unremarkable facts as that urban dwellers tended to hold their capital in forms other than land, that schools tended to be located in towns, and that landless citizens tended to become engineers rather than veterinary surgeons.

There is worse to come. The fact that Protestants tended to live in large towns, and conversely that the inhabitants of large towns tended to be Protestants, is a proposition that held good in Baden and certain other parts of Germany but which is by no means universally applicable. A multitude of historical accidents enter into the equation. At least 90 % of the rural population of the United States are Protestants of one sort or another—insofar as they belong to any church at all. The Catholics live in urban areas, especially the large cities of the eastern states. The 'Puritanism' that is practised in these quarters, particularly by the Irish Catholics, may even be more rigid than Weber's idea of 'real' Puritanism. And as for the

conversion to Protestantism of various groups in Germany—
a quotation from Offenbacher himself is to the point:

'In accordance with the principle "cuius regio, eius religio" the
determining influence was not as a rule the social and religious
convictions of the masses but the religious posture adopted by
the secular ruler, which was conditioned by a combination of
political and strictly spiritual factors and was usually unaffected
by economic considerations.'

This should already have been a clear warning signal to Weber.

The crucial factor determining which school course was
chosen in Baden was—let it be repeated—quite simply the
educational facilities available in the particular district. But this
fact is obscured by the average figures for the country as a
whole, and a false correlation between religious faith and school
attendance creeps in. With the help of this observation the scope
of our criticism of Weber can be enlarged. Weber fell into error
by starting from the assumption that Protestants, especially
Puritans, and Catholics were the real 'primary groups'. The
economic divergences which he thought he had discovered
—and we have seen in the case of Fugger and Alberti how
artificial these often were—are interpreted in terms of religion
as the 'primary factor'.

In just the same way and using exactly the same material
as a base, Weber and his successors could have 'proved' that
geographical or climatic conditions were responsible for the
great economic contrasts. Thus, in recent years northern Europe
has been more prosperous than southern Europe (and incident-
ally Belgium can be accounted for by this theory), while on
the other side of the Atlantic, North America as a whole has
been more prosperous than South America, and the northern
part of North America itself far more prosperous than the
south. Or equally, Weber could have worked on the hypothesis
of the 'Teutonic' and 'Latin' races—generalisations would be
based on degrees of 'contamination' or 'improvement' by blood

146

of other racial stocks: it is all a question of 'ideal types'—and he could thus have 'proved' the Teutons to be cleverer than other races and to have a more 'capitalistic' approach to life.

In fact, in all such 'proofs' we can never escape the absurdities of circular reasoning. In the last analysis, all we can establish is that merchants and manufacturers were more interested in commerce and industry than were landowners and farmers; that many schools in large mercantile cities taught commercial subjects; that a state, province or city where industrialisation was in progress quite soon developed an interest in technical education for children and young persons; that diligent people worked harder, saved more and no doubt went to church more often than the careless and lazy.

Wherever a state turned from Catholicism to Protestantism (whether by royal decree as in England, Scandinavia and many states of Germany, or after a national struggle for liberation as in the Netherlands) we have magnificent raw material for constructing specious correlations and causal connections between Protestantism on the one hand and educational systems and occupational preferences on the other. Sometimes, perhaps, it may even have been that a sovereign's success in shaking off the fetters of Rome proceeded from his country's economic strength, and therewith—in that era of money-hungry mercenary armies—its military strength. In such a case as this —here of course much simplified—the nation in question could be regarded as having become Protestant because it was rich, even though the connection was indirect. But the manner of the transition, it should be noted, is quite different from Robertson's concept of the propagation of religion through economic channels.

In other words, we can produce pretty well whatever correlation or causal connection we like, according as we start from this feature or that as the 'primary' or 'differentiating' factor. The number of possible variations is so large that only one conclusion seems possible: we must refrain, in the interests of truth and common sense, from *all* such generalisations.

147

Weber's hypothesis of a direct correlation between Puritanism and economic progress represents a generalisation which, quite apart from the question of its factual basis, is methodologically inadmissible. The two phenomena are so vague and universal as to be incapable of evaluation by the technique of correlation. Moreover, Weber's own definitions are exceedingly imprecise. 'Protestantism' is used in a variety of different connotations. Sometimes it means Protestantism in general. Even here we run into the difficulty of drawing the boundary with Reformist-flavoured Catholicism. Usually, however, Weber includes in it 'only' Calvinism and the Free Church sects—it is apparent that the strong links between Puritanism and the Lutheran school of thought, through such creeds as Moravianism and Pietism, are to be excluded. Sometimes he speaks of 'original' and sometimes of 'later' Calvinism—but how are these two stages of Calvinism to be distinguished from one another in the context of Weber's theory? Sometimes, like Tawney later, he postulates a Puritanism that is 'true and genuine,' 'Puritan' in a deeper sense and specifically distinct from that of the great Puritan fathers. The fallacy of this gyration has already been demonstrated. Finally, Weber hits on the idea that what he really means is what he calls the secularised Puritanism of Benjamin Franklin. He serenely ignores the fact that the strong influence of Puritanism upon economic development over a span of nearly three hundred years before Franklin, which he himself postulated, thereby becomes difficult to explain.

It is even more impossible, if that were conceivable, to devise any precise definition of the second factor, 'capitalism' and the 'spirit of capitalism'. The very fact that numerous authors have laboured assiduously to make capitalism pedagogically manageable by fabricating such concepts as 'pre-capitalism' and 'mercantile capitalism', not to mention 'pre-capitalistic capitalism' and 'high capitalism', reveals how hazy it all is. There are no clear definitions nor even any reasonably distinct periods to work with. The very fact that, even where the final economic outcome seems to have amounted to the same thing, development did not however pass through the same stages in every country, makes it impossible to define capitalism and its various periods closely. England, Germany, the United States, Russia—the mere mention of these countries proclaims that any sufficiently unambiguous definitions of 'economic growth,' 'capitalism' and 'industrialisation' are impossible. To quote Marc Bloch, capitalism has as many birth certificates as there are historians studying the subject.

Weber himself appears to have sensed this. At all events, it seems probable that it was a feeling of uncertainty in formulating his concepts that caused him to shift from 'capitalism' to 'capitalistic spirit'. He could define the latter pretty much as he liked—using the circular arguments described in chapter II.

Weber worked in terms of what he called 'ideal types'. The very term itself shows that these are theoretical constructions conjured up for the purpose of making simple models, unambiguous in conception, that will elucidate vital themes of social evolution. In principle there is nothing objectionable in this approach. The error lay in the fact that Weber's 'ideal types' were anything but unambiguous in conception. In attempting to make his 'ideal types' faithful to reality and historical truth, he rendered them much too complex to be 'ideal types', thus contravening the principles of the 'model method' and losing sight of the need for firm definition. A model constructed on these eccentric lines was then employed, not as a theoretical structure, but as an interpretation of reality. The resulting explanation could scarcely fail to be pure nonsense.

In the guise of 'ideal types' the Reformation, the later Puritanism and the Free Church sects appeared much more clearly divorced from another 'ideal type', Catholicism, than they were in reality. All transitional forms, everything they had in common, were lost. Differences were grossly exaggerated. The same sort of treatment was given to 'capitalism' and the 'capitalistic

149

spirit' in Puritan countries on the one hand, and to economic life and thought in Catholic countries on the other. Rationalism was depicted as a unique and vital characteristic of Quaker manufacturers in England and Methodist millionaires in the United States. But the highly developed rationalism, in Weber's own meaning, to be found in the Catholic families of Fugger and Brentano was explained away. It was simply declared to be a quite different rationalism from that of the Puritans and Franklin.

The complete arbitrariness of the technique of coupling, of 'correlating', such vaguely defined and in fact indefinable phenomena should be obvious to anyone. It is strange that so many authors after Weber have been able to study his theories without pausing before his basic weakness: the fogginess of the concepts he employs. Perhaps the explanation is that Weber's theories have been universally viewed as a rebuttal of the materialist interpretation of history.

Even aside from the extreme vagueness of his concepts, Weber's method is unwarrantable. There is no justification for isolating, as he did, a single factor in a prolonged and intricate pattern of development—no matter how clearly definable or capable of isolation from other factors—and correlating it with a vast aspect of the whole history of Western civilisation. It is in general a hopeless undertaking to try to isolate one particular factor even from a relatively limited sequence of events, in one particular country and over a very short period of time, with the object of determining the extent to which the factor in question evolved in harmony with the general process under consideration, i.e., the degree of 'correlation' and 'co-variation'. But Weber does not hesitate to embark on such an undertaking for so complex a phenomenon as Puritanism and for so wide a concept as economic development, not over a short period but over about four hundred years, not in a limited geographical region but over the Western world as a whole!

CHAPTER V

Conclusion

'Lay not up for yourselves treasures upon earth, where moth and rust doth corrupt, and where thieves break through and steal: But lay up for yourselves treasures in heaven, where neither moth nor rust doth corrupt, and where thieves do not break through nor steal: For where your treasure is, there will your heart be also.'

These verses from the Sermon on the Mount are fundamental to the Christian outlook. No matter what the church or sect, the guiding principle is the renunciation of the world and the quest for a secure place in the Kingdom of Heaven. The doctrine of predestination, which permeates the whole of Pauline Christianity and was not invented by Calvin or the Puritans, does not alter this fact. On the contrary, it may rather have intensified the sense of estrangement from things temporal and the resolve to lay up treasures in heaven and not on earth. Insofar as wordly affairs claimed any interest, they were measured in terms of eternity and the Kingdom of Heaven. Insofar as economic problems were considered, the aim was to subordinate business and enterprise to a rigorous Christian code of morality that obstructed and confined them. Calvin, Wesley and Baxter did not differ from Paul, Augustine or Thomas Aquinas in this matter.

Mercantilism, the Enlightenment, Darwinism, economic liberalism—all these systems of thought, in which a central

[1] Matthew 6, xix—xxi.

role was played by economic expansion and the belief in a better future for nations or men through the increase of capital and the raising of standard of welfare—cut across all religious creeds, or went over or around them. The elements of these philosophies that were fundamental from the economic point of view were not borrowed from Protestantism and Puritanism but were entirely separate from and unrelated to these religious faiths: rationalism, faith in capitalism and the blessings of capitalism, the demand for untrammelled liberty for—to quote the spokesman of the American mineowners in the coal strike of 1902, George F. Baer—'the Christian men to whom our God in His infinite wisdom has given control of the property interest of the country'.[2]

Although the rationalism of the Enlightenment, the 'survival-of-the-fittest' notions of social Darwinism, and *laissez-faire* liberalism were all able to exhibit themselves to advantage in both the ideological and the practical worlds, this did not always or even usually imply the emancipation of the individual from religious faith, from belief in God the Redeemer. God and Mammon were unconcernedly worshipped at one and the same time, and God was equated with Mammon. Under the environmental influence of wealth, enterprise and speculation—from which the churches too received economic benefits–priests and preachers began to hail capitalists, entrepreneurs and speculators as the elect of God. But it is over-hasty to infer from this that Protestantism and Puritanism created capitalism and capitalists, or were a necessary prerequisite of their rise to a position of dominance. In all religious faiths, the servants of God have invoked Him as a guarantee of the righteousness and prosperity of their own social class, their own nation, their own race—in short their own interests. But we cannot assert that Christianity was therefore the cause of all the oppression of one social class by another that has been committed in God's name, or of all the wars in which the weapons have been blessed by Christian priests, or of all the aggressions perpetrated by repre-

[2] Quoted from F. L. Allen, *op. cit.*, p. 83.

sentatives of the white races upon other peoples in the alleged service of God and the Holy Trinity.

Thus, our scrutiny of Puritan doctrine and capitalist ideology, of the capitalistic spirit that Weber saw personified in Benjamin Franklin and the American captains of industry, has rendered untenable the hypothesis of a connection between Puritanism and capitalism in which religion motivated economics.

Nor have we found Weber's theories tenable in the matter of the special Puritan virtues of diligence and thrift that he postulated. In the first place it is uncertain what role they played in economic expansion at all; secondly, the Puritans were undoubtedly not alone in their endeavour to inculcate diligence and thrift. These virtues were preached as zealously in Catholic France as in Puritan Scotland. Similar considerations have been found to apply to the problem of usury. The approach of Calvin and his successors was not intrinsically different from that of Catholicism; emancipation was achieved independently, as is were, of the religious code. For hundreds of years after the Reformation, in Protestant countries as well as Catholic, the attempt to keep interest rates down and enforce low legal maxima largely continued to find expression in the secular, commercial law dictated by mercantilism. Furthermore, it cannot be determined whether high and freely-moving interest rates promoted economic expansion or whether it was not the contrary phenomenon of low rates of interest that was a more effective force encouraging expansion.

The correlation from which Weber started we have also found dubious, aside from the impossibility, in the last resort, of correlating concepts as broad and vague as those in question. Even if, speaking in quite general terms, Protestant countries did in fact achieve greater economic prosperity than Catholic, it is evident in the first place that the range of variations within the Protestant group, just as in the Catholic group, is very wide, and secondly that the Protestant states have no position of pre-eminence over the Catholic, nor the Puritan states over the rest of the Protestant group.

153

Persons of Free Church and Puritan persuasion have sometimes made outstanding contributions to economic life. But this fact constitutes no justification for linking economic success with religious faith. In many instances there are more plausible explanations, such as special education, family relationships and alien status; or that within the groups subjected to religious persecution it was the merchants who migrated and were received by other countries with particular eagerness and especially good prospects of success; or that the practice of religion and a certain degree of prosperity were associated with a generally industrious personality—and that industriousness was the primary factor. It is plain, however, that in many respects the contribution of Free Church denominations has been violently exaggerated. They formed a quite small element in a broad and general phenomenon, as is shown by an analysis of such factors as the influence of family relationships and the 'role of foreigners' in trade. It is simply that this tiny element is the one that has been particularly noticed.

Thus our conclusion is that, whether we start from the doctrines of Puritanism and 'capitalism' or from the actual concept of a correlation between religion and economic action, we can find no support for Weber's theories. Almost all the evidence contradicts them.

Index

Revised March, 1964

harper ✦ torchbooks

HUMANITIES AND SOCIAL SCIENCES

American Studies

JOHN R. ALDEN: The American Revolution, 1775-1783.† *Illus.* TB/3011

RAY STANNARD BAKER: Following the Color Line: *An Account of Negro Citizenship in the American Democracy.‡ Illus. Introduction by Dewey Grantham, Jr.* TB/3053

RAY A. BILLINGTON: The Far Western Frontier, 1830-1860.† *Illus.* TB/3012

JOSEPH L. BLAU, Ed.: Cornerstones of Religious Freedom in America. *Selected Basic Documents, Court Decisions and Public Statements. Enlarged and revised edition with new Intro. by Editor* TB/118

RANDOLPH S. BOURNE: War and the Intellectuals: *Collected Essays, 1915-1919.‡ Edited with an Introduction by Carl Resek* TB/3043

A. RUSSELL BUCHANAN: The United States and World War II. † *Illus.* Volume I TB/3044
Volume II TB/3045

ABRAHAM CAHAN: The Rise of David Levinsky: *a novel. Introduction by John Higham* TB/1028

JOSEPH CHARLES: The Origins of the American Party System TB/1049

T. C. COCHRAN & WILLIAM MILLER: The Age of Enterprise: *A Social History of Industrial America* TB/1054

FOSTER RHEA DULLES: America's Rise to World Power, 1898-1954.† *Illus.* TB/3021

W. A. DUNNING: Reconstruction, Political and Economic, 1865-1877 TB/1073

CLEMENT EATON: The Growth of Southern Civilization, 1790-1860.† *Illus.* TB/3040

HAROLD U. FAULKNER: Politics, Reform and Expansion, 1890-1900.† *Illus.* TB/3020

LOUIS FILLER: The Crusade against Slavery, 1830-1860.† *Illus.* TB/3029

EDITORS OF FORTUNE: America in the Sixties: *the Economy and the Society. Two-color charts* TB/1015

LAWRENCE HENRY GIPSON: The Coming of the Revolution, 1763-1775.† *Illus.* TB/3007

FRANCIS J. GRUND: Aristocracy in America: *Jacksonian Democracy* TB/1001

OSCAR HANDLIN, Editor: This Was America: *As Recorded by European Travelers to the Western Shore in the Eighteenth, Nineteenth, and Twentieth Centuries. Illus.* TB/1119

MARCUS LEE HANSEN: The Atlantic Migration: 1607-1860. *Edited by Arthur M. Schlesinger; Introduction by Oscar Handlin* TB/1052

MARCUS LEE HANSEN: The Immigrant in American History. *Edited with a Foreword by Arthur Schlesinger, Sr.* TB/1120

JOHN D. HICKS: Republican Ascendancy, 1921-1933.† *Illus.* TB/3041

JOHN HIGHAM, Ed.: The Reconstruction of American History TB/1068

ROBERT H. JACKSON: The Supreme Court in the American System of Government TB/1106

THOMAS JEFFERSON: Notes on the State of Virginia.‡ *Introduction by Thomas Perkins Abernethy* TB/3052

WILLIAM E. LEUCHTENBURG: Franklin D. Roosevelt and the New Deal, 1932-1940.† *Illus.* TB/3025

LEONARD W. LEVY: Freedom of Speech and Press in Early American History: *Legacy of Suppression* TB/1109

ARTHUR S. LINK: Woodrow Wilson and the Progressive Era, 1910-1917.† *Illus.* TB/3023

BERNARD MAYO: Myths and Men: *Patrick Henry, George Washington, Thomas Jefferson* TB/1108

JOHN C. MILLER: The Federalist Era, 1789-1801.† *Illus.* TB/3027

PERRY MILLER & T. H. JOHNSON, Editors: The Puritans: *A Sourcebook of Their Writings* Volume I TB/1093
Volume II TB/1094

GEORGE E. MOWRY: The Era of Theodore Roosevelt and the Birth of Modern America, 1900-1912.† *Illus.* TB/3022

WALLACE NOTESTEIN: The English People on the Eve of Colonization, 1603-1630.† *Illus.* TB/3006

RUSSEL BLAINE NYE: The Cultural Life of the New Nation, 1776-1801.† *Illus.* TB/3026

GEORGE E. PROBST, Ed.: The Happy Republic: *A Reader in Tocqueville's America* TB/1060

FRANK THISTLETHWAITE: America and the Atlantic Community: *Anglo-American Aspects, 1790-1850* TB/1107

---

† The New American Nation Series, edited by Henry Steele Commager and Richard B. Morris.

‡ American Perspectives series, edited by Bernard Wishy and William E. Leuchtenburg.

* The Rise of Modern Europe series, edited by William L. Langer.

** Researches in the Social, Cultural, and Behavioral Sciences, edited by Benjamin Nelson

§ The Library of Religion and Culture, edited by Benjamin Nelson.

Σ Harper Modern Science Series, edited by James R. Newman.

º Not for sale in Canada.